Every Young Adult's
BREAKUP
SURVIVAL
GUIDE

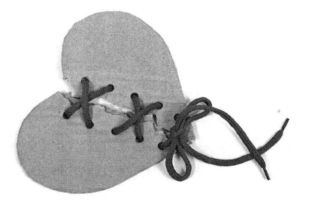

Tips, Tricks & Expert Advice
for Recovering

EVERY YOUNG ADULT'S BREAKUP SURVIVAL GUIDE: TIPS, TRICKS & EXPERT ADVICE FOR RECOVERING

Copyright © 2015 Atlantic Publishing Group, Inc.
1405 SW 6th Avenue • Ocala, Florida 34471 • Phone 800-814-1132 • Fax 352-622-1875
Website: www.atlantic-pub.com • E-mail: sales@atlantic-pub.com
SAN Number: 268-1250

Library of Congress Cataloging-in-Publication Data

Names: Atlantic Publishing Group.
Title: Every young adult's breakup survival guide : tips, tricks & expert
  advice for recovering / by Atlantic Publishing Group, Inc.
Other titles: Breakup survival guide
Description: Ocala, Florida : Atlantic Publishing Group, Inc., 2015. |
  Audience: Grade 9 to 12. | Includes bibliographical references and index.
Identifiers: LCCN 2015035611| ISBN 9781601389855 (alk. paper) | ISBN
  160138985X (alk. paper)
Subjects: LCSH: Dating (Social customs)--Juvenile literature. | Teenage
  girls--Attitudes--Juvenile literature. | Love--Juvenile literature. |
  Separation (Psychology)--Juvenile literature. | Interpersonal
  relations--Juvenile literature.
Classification: LCC HQ801 .E97 2015 | DDC 306.73--dc23 LC record available at http://lccn.loc.
gov/2015035611

Printed on Recycled Paper

Printed in the United States

Reduce. Reuse.
RECYCLE.

A decade ago, Atlantic Publishing signed the Green Press Initiative. These guidelines promote environmentally friendly practices, such as using recycled stock and vegetable-based inks, avoiding waste, choosing energy-efficient resources, and promoting a no-pulping policy. We now use 100-percent recycled stock on all our books. The results: in one year, switching to post-consumer recycled stock saved 24 mature trees, 5,000 gallons of water, the equivalent of the total energy used for one home in a year, and the equivalent of the greenhouse gases from one car driven for a year.

Over the years, we have adopted a number of dogs from rescues and shelters. First there was Bear and after he passed, Ginger and Scout. Now, we have Kira, another rescue. They have brought immense joy and love into not just into our lives, but into the lives of all who met them.

We want you to know a portion of the profits of this book will be donated in Bear, Ginger and Scout's memory to local animal shelters, parks, conservation organizations, and other individuals and nonprofit organizations in need of assistance.

– Douglas & Sherri Brown,
President & Vice-President of Atlantic Publishing

Table of Contents

Chapter 5: How to Not Let Yourself Go Mentally..................117

Chapter 6: How to Not Let Yourself Go Physically 143

Chapter 7: Getting Support From Others 157

How to Have a Healthy Breakup

Even if breaking up is the right thing to do, it is not easy. Here are some tips that can help you get through your breakup, no matter what side you are on:

- **You can cry.** Even if you think of yourself as tough, the emotional pain you are going through can bring anyone to tears. You might also want to call or text a friend or family member to offer you a literal shoulder on which to cry. You need to accept that it is fine to feel bad about the end of your relationship.

- **Find new things to do.** Now is the time to take the art class you have been thinking about or try to make your way through all of the *Harry Potter* movies. Maybe you can enroll in a taekwondo class or join a hockey team.

Being depressed makes you want to sit around and mope, but resist the urge. The more you are active, the more things you will find to fill the emotional hole your ex left.

- **Talk to other people.** Try not to wear out your friends and family, but do not keep your feelings to yourself. Talk to other people and get those feelings off your chest. However, you will want to watch what you say, especially if you have mutual friends. You can talk about how you feel the relationship was not working, but do not badmouth your ex. Be as honest as possible. Keep your opinions and drama off Facebook, Twitter, Vine, etc.

- **Be optimistic.** Do not give in to the negative feelings you experience during a breakup. Instead of dwelling on the past relationship, look forward to the next one. If you alter the way you think, you can change the way you feel, which will change the way you act. When you finally feel optimistic, you can free yourself to accomplish new goals, try new things, and start to live life to its fullest again.

f you are reading this book, you are likely getting over a recent bout of heartbreak. Also likely is that, whatever happened, it was painful. Perhaps your relationship dissolved in one huge fight. Perhaps it just faded slowly, until you and your partner woke up one morning and discovered that after all you had been through, you did not love each other anymore. Maybe your partner said one final, hateful remark that burrowed its way into your heart and kicked down your self-confidence. Maybe you two tried to end on good terms and promised, that no matter what, you would remain friends.

Regardless, you are likely alone now. Depending on the time frame, you could still be at the stage in which you have inadvertently memorized the television schedule. Or you could be out, going to school, going to concerts, and acting as though everything is alright. Chances are, you have friends who have also had their share of heartbreak, and you might be thinking of them and remembering how they were sad before hanging out with you and other friends. You are wondering if they were that well adjusted or if they are like you and put on a brave front. You might even try to convince yourself you are all right and rebound into another relationship but still think of your ex.

Whatever your situation, getting your heart broken is painful. Dealing with that sudden void where someone special used to be is not easy, and even people who seem to get past the depression heartbreak causes still find themselves with periods where they are reminded they used to be in a relationship. During a weak moment, you might wonder whether you will ever get over this heartbreak and get on with your life again.

That is where this book comes in. You will receive help on how to get through your breakup and the resulting heartache, and how to recover your life again as you emerge with renewed hopes and dreams.

We will start with the dissolution of the relationship and will discuss the stages of how a relationship ends and map out what happens at each stage. We will also take a look at the methods people use when they break up. That will lead us to look at the Five Stages of Loss — denial, anger, bargaining, depression and acceptance — and talk about how you can deal with each one. From there is a guide on how to detach yourself from your ex. You will learn the best way to separate yourself, the excuses you make to see your ex again and why they are not good ideas, and how to share news of the breakup with your family and friends.

We will also cover the tricky subject of dealing with your break-up on social media sites.

You will likely have to be around your ex at some point. You might have similar social circles and still share friends. Because you might have conflicting ideas on how to behave, Chapter 4 will cover how to be on your best behavior, why that is important, and will show you unhealthy behaviors to avoid. Because you might have an ex who has no intentions of being on his or her best behavior, this chapter will also cover how to handle an ex who is behaving badly or in ways that make you worry about your mental or physical well-being. Also, because one of the common goals of heartbreak victims is to preserve the friendship, this chapter will discuss the benefits and drawbacks of trying to be friends with your ex with the goal most separated couples eventually consider — reconciling with each other.

You will also need to keep busy after you have broken up with someone, so you will learn how to fill the void your ex left in your life. This chapter will explain why you need to keep busy and features a comprehensive overview of how to figure out what you want to do, even if you feel like doing nothing. Chapters 5 and 6 will discuss how to maintain yourself physically and mentally. Diet, exercise and positive thinking are covered.

The support of your friends and family is also a way to cope with your heartbreak. You will find out how to get support from your friends and your family, and how to do so without wearing them down. This chapter will cover determining the point when you need to seek professional help, what to expect in therapy, and how to find a suitable therapist. Because you might be placed in group therapy as part of your treatment, you will also learn how it works and how to behave.

After you have weathered the worst of your heartbreak, you can start to think about regaining your hopes and dreams. The first thing you will need to do is take stock of your life and set some goals, and in Chapter 8 you will learn how by finding out the areas in which you are happy and the areas on which you want to work. Because organizing your thoughts is a key step in taking stock of your life, this chapter will also show you how to create lists. You will get guidelines on how to make lists that are useful to you and advice on how to thoroughly analyze and realize what you want to work on.

Once you have taken stock of your life, you can start to set goals. You will learn how to ensure your goals are realistic, then figure out the first steps that will put you on your way to achieving those goals.

Chapter 9 focuses on finding and meeting new people. You will find ideas for where to look for new friendships or relationships. Because not everyone is gifted in the art of chatting people up, a crash course in how to strike up a conversation and keep it going is provided. This section ends with one of the most difficult parts of any new relationship — asking out the other person.

Asking out another person means you are ready to begin a new relationship, and that is what the final chapter will cover.

You will learn when is the right time to move on, why you should not start your search for a romantic partner too soon, and what problems can arise in rebound relationships. Perhaps most important, you will learn how to avoid sabotaging your new relationship, such as raising your standards too high, and why to not compare your new boy- or girlfriend with your ex.

BUT MY RELATIONSHIP IS DIFFERENT!

Most of the time, books that offer relationship advice talk about getting over relationships from the viewpoint of a girlfriend getting over a boyfriend, or a boyfriend getting over a girlfriend. But what if you are not in that kind of relationship? Will this book help you, too?

This book is for you, no matter what kind of relationship you have, and regardless of whether you are heterosexual, homosexual, bisexual, male, or female. You may be looking at this book and wondering if it will even offer you any advice you can use. Rest assured, this book is built for you, no matter what your relationship. No matter how different you think your relationship might be, human beings go through similar reactions and stages. Loss is universal. So is recovering from it. No matter how far along you were in your relationship when you got your heart broken or what kind of relationship it was, there is something in this book for you. Believe it or not, we are all in this together.

Chapter 1

Understanding How a Relationship Fails

Getting your heart broken raises questions. Why did he or she leave? What could I have done to prevent this? Will I ever see the stuff I left at his or her place again?

One common question, though, is, "How did this happen?" People try to figure out how their relationship fell apart, and this question cannot be answered. Researchers Steve Duck and Julia Wood studied the process of falling out of love in 2006 and 2007. From their studies, they came up with what they call the "Death Cycle of Relationships," a companion of sorts to their model of the stages involved in building up a relationship.

While friendships might end in different ways, the process of falling out of love is consistent.

Falling out of love starts with a phase called the **intrapsychic processes**, in which one or both people in the relationship are aware of the relationship's problems. During this phase, focusing on the relationship's negative parts might lead to more negative thoughts about the relationship. In time, this affects the person's outlook of the relationship. The intrapsychic stage is also when the people in the relationship begin thinking about other relationships they could be having. This is the stage where you start to feel his constant lateness is less of a cute personality quirk and more of a sign that he feels your relationship is less of a priority than his friends or hobbies. This is where you start to realize that when she teases you in front of your friends, she is being mean.

CONFLICT IN ROMANTIC RELATIONSHIPS

One of the worst ways to break up with someone is to say something in the middle of a fight that you cannot take back. The better you are at handling conflict, the smoother your relationship will be, and if you do have to break up with your partner, you can take comfort in the knowledge that you handled your conflict well, even if you do not end up together. To that end, here is quick advice to help you constructively handle those conflicts that indicate something is wrong with your relationship.

Before the discussion:

- Before you begin talking with your partner about a conflict, calm down. Talking about the conflict when you are upset or angry can result in destructive communication and regret afterward.

- Make sure your partner is ready to discuss the problem with you. If your significant other does not want to talk, no constructive communication can take place.

- Schedule time to talk about the conflict. Give yourself time or set up time to cool down.

- After you have scheduled a time for the discussion, know your goal. It might be nice to win the argument, but you do not want your partner to feel like he or she has lost.

- Find out what your partner's goal is in this discussion.

- Plan to discuss the conflict in a private place. No one likes seeing couples argue publicly, least of all the couple themselves.

- Plan to have enough time to properly discuss the conflict because it is hard to give your full attention to something when you have a quickly approaching deadline or sports match.

During the discussion:

- Frame the discussion in a way that each person gains something. Think about what you want to get out of the discussion and how your partner can benefit from it. For instance, if you want your partner to be more punctual, you can frame your goal by saying, "I wish you would not be late for our dates. The later you are for a date, the less time we can spend together. It also seems to make us stressed, which detracts from the time we spend together. Is there a way we can work to increase your punctuality and decrease the stress in both our lives?"

- Listen to what your partner says. At first, do not try to launch a counterargument. Understand his point of view, and be sure to convey that you are listening to what he is saying.

- To let your partner know you are listening, calmly paraphrase his arguments. Your partner will be happy that you seem to understand what he has to say, and this technique is a way to force yourself to process your partner's statements. Keep your tone non-condescending and non-judgmental.

When you get a chance to talk, use words that show you value the other person and that you want to cooperate with him. For instance, you can say, "I think we should..." or "You have a point." Also, use "I" statements to convey how you feel instead of blame-placing "you" statements. Instead of saying, "You do not respect me when you make me wait for a long time," say, "I feel that you do not respect my time when you are late and I have gone to the effort of being on time."

Resolve the conflict:

- Value everyone involved in the conflict and their points of contention. This includes you and your partner and the relationship itself.

- To manage the conflict so it can be constructive, validate how your partner feels. If you find out what is causing him to be late, you can come up with a solution that will not make him feel insulted but will make you feel you have made your feelings known.

The way you handle this conflict will strengthen the relationship as you set new parameters and learn more about each other. Perhaps you agree to give him a 20-minute warning call, or he agrees to call you a half-hour before you are scheduled to meet. The best conclusion is where you feel respected.

If you do not value or understand your partner's point of view, it can lead to a bad outcome. You might slip into a "win-lose" scenario, in which you want to win the conflict. In this case, it would be forcing him to be punctual by harping on his perceived immaturity and irresponsibility, followed up by threats of doing things by yourself and not inviting him if he is going to be late. You might win the conflict and get your partner to be punctual, but he will be aware he has lost the conflict. That, and the relationship has changed. You have established yourself as the more dominant force in this conflict, and you have shown your partner that you see your views as more important. This is all right as long as your partner does not have the same view.

If your partner feels as strongly about the issue as you do, the scenario can deteriorate into a lose-lose. In this scenario, you walk away unsatisfied. The issue is unlikely to be resolved, and even if it is, the relationship itself is damaged because neither of you walk away feeling your opinions matter to the other person.

Grace is another important part of valuing all aspects of the relationship. Show grace after conflicts, especially when you are in the right. If your partner admits she was in the wrong and wants to work with you to correct her behavior, work with her and then put the incident behind you. For instance, if you have had a conflict with your partner about not helping to clean the kitchen after you cook together and she agrees this is a problem, do not harp on her previous failure by saying, "We need to clean the kitchen after dinner," or, "Do I need to remind you to clean the kitchen?" If you are going to say anything, say, "Let's clean the kitchen and then watch TV," or "Need help cleaning the kitchen?" If you want to be graceful, clean the kitchen by yourself if she forgets to before she leaves. Displaying thoughtfulness and forgiveness can go a long way in showing your commitment to a relationship, and in this scenario, your partner is likely to be touched by the gesture.

If the problems the intrapsychic processes unearthed are not solved, the exclusive nature of the relationship — complete with inside jokes begins to deteriorate. At this point, the decay of the relationship moves into the **dyadic process**. This is one of the important points of a relationship breakdown because couples start to neglect areas of their relationship they once maintained. These areas involve communication. Because women tend to become less happy with a relationship the more communication in the relationship deteriorates, this stage can be detrimental to women. The dyadic process affects men because men become unhappy in a relationship when treasured routines and behaviors go away. This is where the clichéd phrase, "We do not talk anymore" comes from.

The dyadic process stage is when each partner should be aware that there are problems with the relationship. According to Steve Duck's research, these problems should be addressed. This is the stage at which the relationship can be saved, but the people involved must be willing to discuss the rough spots in their relationship (in other words, address the issues), possess the ability to communicate enough with each other to understand each other's problems, and be committed enough to save the relationship. If the relationship cannot be saved, the relationship fails, and each partner must deal with the final stages on his or her own.

During the **social support** stage, each person in the relationship turns to other people for support as their relationship collapses. People look to their family or friends. This is the stage of the breakup that draws in other people. These outside friends dread their involvement in a breakup between two friends. The reason is that during this stage of the relationship breakdown, each person in the former relationship desires — perhaps even needs — sympathy and support from other people. People in a dissolving relationship might also want to avoid being embarrassed by their actions or thoughts before the breakup; as a result, both parties portray themselves in the best possible light. They might also give less-than-flattering accounts of their exes, regardless of how it might come back to haunt them in the future. This stage can be wearisome for mutual friends of the former couple because the friends feel pressured to choose between one person and the other. This can result in the loss of a friend.

After the talking has been done and the issues have been pondered, each member of the relationship is finally ready for the second-to-last phase in the relationship's death. The **grave-dressing process** is named that because at this point, people bury the relationship and start to accept its loss. Mourning is common at this point, and almost everyone is introspective to a degree, thinking about the wonderful parts of the relationship and perhaps even imagining what might have been. Although this kind of reflection can be seen as a refusal to move on with your life, it is considered healthy, provided the reflective period does not last so long that people start to dwell on their thoughts. According to studies James Honeycutt in 2003 and Colleen Saffrey and Marion Ehrenberg in 2007 conducted, the more you reflect on your breakup, the more likely you are to become depressed and deal with the break up more negatively than someone who only reflects on the former relationship for a little while and then moves on.

The final part of the relationship death cycle is a happy one. The **resurrection process** is when both people are "reborn" and consider themselves single again. They are able to move on with their lives. They begin to reorganize their lives to compensate for the loss of the ex-partner, and they start to do things as a single person and even look to establish another romantic connection.

MIX-AND-MATCH STRATEGIES

Throughout the breakup strategies discussed, you might be replaying the events of your breakup in your mind and trying to discover the strategy used to exit your relationship. Do not be surprised if the method used in your relationship does not resemble one strategy.

People use multiple strategies to break up with someone. They switch strategies to make their point. For instance, if a woman uses the **avoidance** strategy, she might go for the **direct dump** when her boyfriend spots her in the hallway at school and confronts her about her behavior. Other times, they might adjust their strategies based on the reaction of the other person, such as when an ex begins to cry during the justification strategy and the dumper switches to the **positive tone** strategy to make the ex feel better.

Breakup Strategies

A common reaction to heartbreak is to try to figure out what happened. Why did he list all the things I did wrong when he did not make a big deal out of them before? Why was she nice to me and tell me what a good guy I was before leaving forever? Did he think not seeing me for two weeks was a relationship-ending strategy? Although cataloging the mindset of every couple that breaks up is impossible, determining how someone broke up with you is easier and might shed some light on the things your ex did when he or she broke up with you.

Despite what Paul Simon claims, there are only about 13 ways to leave your lover. Each of these strategies falls into one of four categories, based on two conditions, according to one of the premier researchers in the field of breaking up, Leslie A. Baxter. According to her research, the first condition is who wants out of the relationship. If the breakup is initiated because one person wants out of the relationship, then the breakup is considered **unilateral**. Less common is that both people in the relationship realize they are no longer interested in maintaining the relationship. This is a **bilateral** breakup.

The second condition is whether the breakup will be **direct** or **indirect**. This is the part that draws interest from people because it determines how the breakup will occur. The indirect method of breaking up can take different forms. This might be accomplished by completely shutting down all forms of communication, including not answering telephone calls and ignoring texts. Or, the person who wants the breakup might leave subtle hints, such as reducing affection down to the occasional hug or going out with friends instead of spending time with his or her partner, in the hopes that the other person picks up on the hints. Then there is the direct method of breaking up. Unlike the indirect method, the direct method is straightforward and hard, if not impossible, to misunderstand. Tell the other person point-blank that you are breaking up with him or her. Decide that given the problems you are having, it is time to end the relationship and put everything into a "state of the relationship" speech. Or just state that the relationship is done, without giving any reason why.

These conditions and methods combine in four ways, with each way having different approaches.

Bilateral indirect strategies

This has only one strategy associated with it — the **fadeaway**.

THE FADEAWAY

[Silence]

This is a quiet way of breaking up, when the couple grows apart. This is common during long-distance relationships, and during a fadeaway, a talk about the relationship might not be necessary; the couple might sense the relationship is over. This is the type of situation where the hot guy you made out with at basketball camp just fades from memory, even though the two of you promised you would see each other again. It could also be when, after calls to your girlfriend in dance camp, you realize that keeping in touch with her becomes less frequent. So when you find someone else to date, calling your girlfriend to break up is just a formality.

Bilateral direct strategies

A breakup where both people feel the relationship needs to end has two strategies associated with it.

THE BLAME GAME

"You're such a slob — I can't believe you haven't gotten me sick."

"Just go ahead and yell at me. I guess that's what you're best at."

"I don't know why I ever thought you were worth dating."

"Same here."

In the **blame game**, partners shift the responsibility for the dying relationship onto each other and blame the other person for the relationship's death. This continues after the relationship has ended because even the reasons the relationship has ended are argued over. This type of breakup can get extremely messy, and the people in the relationship rarely end with positive feelings toward each other. However, this strategy provides each partner with a reason to end the relationship, and blaming the end of the relationship on the other person helps each side not have to admit he or she might have been at fault, letting him or her save face.

THE NEGOTIATED BREAKUP

"This isn't working."

"No...it's not. I'm sorry."

"Me too."

A healthier breakup strategy is what Baxter names the **negotiated farewell**. This strategy is similar to the blame game because both sides realize the relationship has what Hollywood couples refer to as "irreconcilable differences." Instead of blaming the other person, however, the partners instead negotiate how to leave the relationship, with each person wanting to be as fair to the other person as possible. The goal of couples engaged in the negotiated farewell is to leave the relationship on a high note, with positive feelings toward each other. Issues covered might be how to coexist with each other in social circles. Only couples that have been close for a long time or in a long-term, committed relationship use this technique.

HOW LONG IS A LONG TIME?

In the negotiated farewell strategy of leaving, you might be asking yourself, "How long is a long time?" When someone is involved in a long-term relationship, how long is that? The answer is hard to define. A reliable definition, though, is when two people have been together long enough to reach the stage of a relationship known as "emotional attachment," according to researcher Helen Fisher at Rutgers University. Unlike the "romantic feelings" stage of the relationship, when your heart and hormones run wild, and the "physical attraction" stage, known as being lovesick, the emotional attachment stage is when you realize your partner is not perfect, and the good outweighs the bad. Reaching this stage does not happen immediately, nor does it happen at the same pace. But as a rule of thumb, a relationship that has lasted for one year or longer is a long-term relationship.

Unilateral indirect strategies

When one person wants to get out of a relationship and does not want the potential confrontation that can ignite during a breakup talk, they might employ one of three potential strategies.

AVOIDANCE

"I'd love to spend time with you, but I just can't. I've got a project I have to work on that's taking up a lot of my time, then I have to visit my grandparents, and after that I promised my brother I'd help him work on his car. I know I haven't talked to you in the past week. Sorry. Goodbye."

The **avoidance** strategy is simple. Avoid him or her and shut down all lines of communication. The idea is that when your partner sees you are actively avoiding all attempts at talking with him or her, he or she will understand the relationship has ended and get on with life. This breakup strategy is used when one person simply wants to end the relationship and does not foresee any friendship with the other person in the future. Additionally, it is used more in low-risk relationships, when the people in the relationship have few formal ties to each another, and when the person breaking up does not have a positive opinion of his or her partner. But this strategy rarely works as well as the person doing it would hope. Avoidance presumes that your soon-to-be ex understands you perfectly or that he or she can read your mind. If your partner does not hear from you, he or she is more likely to want to find out why you have not talked to him or her than he or she is to understand you want to break up. Eventually, the person doing the breaking up will have to say something to get the point across.

COST ESCALATION

"I saw that movie we were supposed to see Friday with someone else. And you need to get a new phone charger. I borrowed yours yesterday and my dog chewed it up."

Another strategy is called **cost escalation**. This entails worsening your behavior by becoming meaner and more inconsiderate to your partner, thereby making him or her think favorably of breaking up with you. This is the least used of all the breakup strategies. Ironically, this can be beneficial to both parties in the relationship. When the person whom you are trying to break up with breaks up with you first, the relationship ends with both sides feeling better about the choice they made to end the relationship. Your ex feels he or she got out of a relationship that was steadily worsening, and you do not have to live with the guilt of breaking his or her heart.

PSEUDO DE-ESCALATION

"I'm just saying we should be friends, not boyfriend and girlfriend. Things have been hard between us, and they weren't when we were friends. So if we go back to being friends, we can still be happy without getting on each other's nerves."

The final unilateral indirect strategy is **pseudo de-escalation**. This indirect method of breaking up is when one partner tries to de-escalate the relationship from romantic to platonic, or at least to not being as close as they were before. This can be anything from a "let's just be friends" speech to "let's take a break from the relationship" speech.

Unilateral direct strategies

DIRECT DUMP

"I want to break up."

This is more familiar territory. One person wants out of the relationship, and he or she expresses problems and concerns to the other person. At its core, the **direct dump** strategy sums up the unilateral direct strategy. This approach is when one person in a relationship approaches the other and announces that he or she wants to end the relationship. The person using the direct dump will have an argument as to why the breakup is preferable to remaining in the relationship and offer the other person no choice but to agree to end the relationship. According to Baxters' research, 81 percent of the people who were broken up with using the direct dump accepted the breakup without putting up a fight, which suggests the advantage of using such a strong message. However, this strategy can be rough for the person on the receiving end because he or she suddenly is told the relationship has ended and has no choice in the matter. The direct dump is used after other, more subtle breakup strategies have failed.

JUSTIFICATION

"When we first got together, we were freshmen; we both wanted to go to college and we had the same interests. But we've both changed. You didn't get into college and worked at a grocery store, and I'm involved with getting my engineering degree. You're more interested in video games, and I joined that book club. We don't talk about anything anymore, and you're not interested in being more mature, and I'm just too involved in school to be romantic with someone right now. Do you see why I think we should break up?"

The **justification** strategy is similar to the direct dump, but with justification, the person breaking up explains to the other person why he or she is ending the relationship. He or she might discuss the changes in the relationship both sides have gone through and the faults of both people in the relationship. Justifying the breakup is one of the best ways to get the other person to understand the relationship is over. This strategy is employed when the people involved have an intimate, committed relationship. It can also lead to a positive outcome for the breakup. The people involved still feel loss, but now they understand what led to the dissolution of the relationship. Unfortunately, there can be a dark side to the justification strategy. If the person breaking off the relationship focuses on the faults and shortcomings of the other person as the reasons why the relationship failed, a positive end to the relationship is unlikely to happen. The other person will get his or her feelings hurt and likely have a lowered self-esteem.

DATES WITH OTHER PEOPLE

"I just need a break from you. I'm going on a date this weekend, and I think you should find someone else to date, too. I just need to see what else is out there. I'm not sure where we stand with each other right now."

The **dates with other people** breakup strategy is less clear on the status of the relationship after the announcement. The person

who initiates this strategy says he or she would like to start dating other people and encourages his or her partner to start dating
other people, too. The other party is not likely to understand this
strategy. It also imposes the will of the person breaking up on his
or her partner without the partner having any input in the matter. The bright side of this strategy is that the person initiating
the breakup is interested in taking a break from a relationship,
particularly if it is intimate and intense. In this case, the relationship can eventually start up again. However, this is often used to
break up permanently.

DE-ESCALATION

"Things just aren't going that well. So let's take a break from each
other. We can still be friends. We can still have lunch together, but
shouldn't we see if we might be happier apart? If we still have
feelings for each other at the end of three months, we can get back
together, all right?"

A related strategy is **de-escalation**. In this strategy, the person
wanting to break up suggests that the relationship takes a step
back. As opposed to pseudo de-escalation, actual de-escalation
comes clean about the fact that this is a breakup of sorts, even as
the person talking about de-escalation talks about seeing if the
relationship can survive the split. This still leaves the possibility of reconciliation in the other person's mind, although rarely
does the reconciliation ever take place.

THREATS AND BULLYING

"I don't know why I dated you. You are so spineless. I am breaking up with you, and you better go along with it. I still have those

pictures of you. Would you like to see them posted on the Internet? Do you think our friends will still look at you the same way? While we are at it, if I hear you tell anyone I was mean to you, I can print those pictures and send them to your parents."

Threats and bullying is a less positive strategy, with a name that says exactly what the person who wants the breakup does to his or her partner. Although this might include threats of what the person will do to the other if he or she refuses to accept the breakup, it also includes threatening his or her partner about his or her behavior after the relationship — for instance, promising revenge on the partner if he or she divulges any embarrassing information about him or her. This is a destructive type of breakup. It wrecks any chance of a friendship afterward and makes the partner feel powerless, which is likely, given the usual loss of self-esteem at the end of a relationship. Another possibility is that the partner might counter the initial threats with threats of his or her own, leading to other negative outcomes.

RELATIONSHIP TRICK TALK

"We just don't agree on anything anymore. You like to watch TV marathons, and I like to exercise. We argue all the time about where to eat, what to eat and even whose turn it is to pick up the bill. I want to solve these problems, but now that I've said all that, it seems like the best thing to do might just be to break up."

The **relationship trick talk** is related to the justification strategy, only less direct. It starts with the partner who wants to break up telling his or her partner he or she would like to discuss problems in the relationship and solve them. However, this talk leads the person doing the breaking up to the conclusion that the relationship's problems are unsolvable and the only strategy is to break up. Because the talk is initiated by the person wanting the breakup, he or she has control of the conversation and can structure it to steer his or her partner toward the conclusion that the only possible solution is to break up. If this strategy goes well, both people in the relationship walk away feeling that they tried to save the relationship, even though breaking up was the best thing to do. If it does not go well, the partner can feel betrayed or manipulated. According to Baxter's research, 27 percent of the breakups observed in the study involved a partner using the relationship trick talk.

POSITIVE TONE

"We had fun. The problem is that we want different things out of life. You're a wonderful person, and I don't think you will have any problem with finding someone who is everything you want. It's just not me."

One unilateral direct breakup strategy, the **positive tone** method, is designed to make the person who is being dumped feel better about the relationship. Although one of the common lines used in this strategy is, "It's not you, it's me," the positive tone strategy can also encompass the person breaking up telling his or her partner that he or she loved the relationship while it lasted, that he or she will find someone else who loves him or her, or that he or she has other priorities that would make a relationship with him or her impossible to sustain. Although this strategy is a direct one, the person being dumped might still interpret the positive tone to mean the relationship could be rekindled or resurfaced at a later date. A person who uses this strategy needs to be clear the breakup is permanent to be successful.

WHAT IS THE BEST WAY TO BREAK UP?

During this discussion of breakup strategies, you might find yourself wondering if there is an ideal way to break up with someone. Strategies, such as the indirect ones, are almost guaranteed to hurt your partner unless both of you want to end the relationship and do not want to be direct about it. Direct is better, although even the justification and positive tone strategies have their downsides. The best advice is to treat your ex the way you would want to be treated. Have the courtesy to break up with your partner the same way.

After reading this, you will have a better idea of how your relationship ended. Even if you were the one who initiated the breakup, you should have a better sense of what happened between you and your ex. Simply understanding the process does not make the outcome any easier, though. The question is, how do you deal with the grief you carry?

Chapter 2

Coping With Grief

A fter suffering from a significant loss, the natural reaction is to feel grief that can rival levels people feel when someone close to them has died. This is understandable and is expected. According to current psychological studies, people who are diagnosed with a terminal illness or who suffer a catastrophic loss go through five stages of grieving. Since psychiatrist Elisabeth Kübler-Ross first introduced this concept in 1969, the five stages are known as the **Kübler-Ross model**. People do not have to be dying or be close to someone dying to experience these stages. Getting your heart broken is loss enough.

Denial

The first stage of the Kübler-Ross model is **denial**. This stage is refusing to accept the relationship is over. It is easier to deny the relationship is finished if your ex has not been direct about breaking up with you. For instance, if she wants to date other people, you can easily convince yourself she just wants a change of pace and will come back to you. If he wants to de-escalate the relationship, you can convince yourself he just needs his space. However, people have been known to still be in denial about an ex who is plainly stating his or her desire to break up.

Denial comes in three flavors. The first is called **simple denial**, which is straightforwardly denying that something has happened. "He didn't break up with me. He just said he was going to date other people." This is the most straightforward means of denial, but it is also hard for someone to convince himself or herself that something simply did not happen. This method of denial is commonly used when someone is confronted with a serious trauma, such as rape or a terminal illness.

Another common means of denial is **minimization**. This stage admits, "Something happened, but it cannot be as serious as it appears." Someone in this type of denial might think, "She said she was breaking up with me, but she didn't mean it. She's just showing me how serious she is about me being late to pick her up."

Then there is the state of denial known as **projections**. At this stage, you admit the facts and their seriousness, but instead of accepting responsibility, you project it onto someone else — in this case, your ex. This is rarely used when trying to deny that a breakup has happened, although it might be used when thinking about who was responsible for the breakup.

Eventually, though, the denial stage ends. It has to end because continuing to deny it flies in the face of reality. Although a person might be able to live in denial about some things, such as the reason he failed a test or that he is overweight, living in denial about something such as a breakup will only last until his former love starts dating other people. Then he will have to face reality either because he does so on his own or because his denial of the facts leads to a confrontation. Unfortunately, facing the situation as it is requires delving into the following stages, which are in the negative end of the emotional spectrum.

Anger

The next stage of the Kübler-Ross model is **anger**. The anger that people feel at the end of a relationship is the kind of anger that arises when someone feels deliberately treated unfairly or harmed by someone else. Someone in this stage will be constantly asking why this loss is happening to him or her. He or she will also start to question why other people are not feeling this kind of loss, or if they are, why it is not affecting them as much. This leads to him or her being consumed with anger and envy. This means that the anger one feels at losing a relationship is projected on others, instead of being directed at himself or herself or at the ex.

When someone is angry, he or she might express it in one of two ways: aggressively or passively. **Aggressive anger** entails the results you would expect, from threatening others — verbally or non-verbally — and bullying other people up to and including physical violence. Aggressive anger can also be expressed by wanting to destroy something, whether it is an object, such as a dish or an urge to harm someone else. The destructive urge might be expressed by destroying other things, such as a relationship between two people or a friendship between the angry person and an acquaintance. People who express their anger aggressively might also be very selfish.

However, someone might also aggressively express their anger by being manic and theatrical, as though they possess more energy than they know how to handle. They might go on a spending spree or channel their anger into a marathon exercise session or long study sessions.

Passive anger, on the other hand, is not expressed as directly as aggressive anger. You might know it by its other name — passive aggression. It can show itself as the person performs saint-like acts of self-sacrifice, acting as though he or she is suffering and eating up the gratefulness he or she receives for his or her actions or refusing help entirely, preferring to be seen as a martyr. He or she might also criticize themselves in public, apologizing for things that are not even his or her fault, and all but openly invite people to criticize him or her, inviting people to martyr him or her in front of others. People who display their anger passively might also become evasive, avoiding conflict and backing down from crises. They might even exhibit a phobia of conflict.

Less publicly, passive anger can display itself as being obsessive, by making sure things are done perfectly, and trying to apply standards of perfection to activities better done in moderation, such as dieting or exercising. The effects of passive anger might also express themselves as ineffectualness, where the person with anger issues sets themselves up for failure through mechanisms — ignoring serious issues while focusing on insignificant issues, relying on people who are not reliable, or being prone to having accidents. Perhaps the ultimate expression of passive anger is where it becomes dispassionate, as the person abandons all feeling and spends more time with objects or intellectual hobbies instead of interacting with people. When someone who is dispassionate with anger has to interact with others, his or her emotions are insincere. He or she tends to not respond to other people's emotions well and lets other people take charge of problems while he or she sits on the sidelines.

Passive anger is as destructive as aggressive anger. Psychological manipulation is one example, when a person provokes other people to be aggressive and then feigns innocence. He or she might undercut people, subtly insult them — "That dress makes you look less fat than that dress you wore yesterday" — or talk behind other people's backs, gossiping or submitting anonymous complaints to teachers or administrators. In extreme cases, this type of manipulation can even entail stealing from others and trying to deceive them.

After reading these ways to express anger, you might be feeling as though someone who feels angry is an absolute monster waiting to be unleashed on an unsuspecting world. The truth is that everyone feels angry, and breakups are a time when feelings of anger surface. Also, few people use these ways to express their anger, whether it is aggressive or passive.

In a breakup, the person who has been dumped is likely going to be furious with his or her ex, and his or her anger might expand to include other people, such as the ex's family and friends. He or she might also take his or her anger out on friends, family and acquaintances. It is during this time that the person going through anger is left to rage at the world and everyone in it. People offering help or comfort at this stage might find themselves the target of insults or accusations — things the person will regret when he or she has calmed down.

TALES OF REVENGE

Many popular urban legends told on the Internet have to do with people getting revenge on their exes or ways a person ended a relationship. There is the woman who sold her ex-husband's sports car for $100 because her husband wanted her to sell it and give him half the money, the ex-husband who filled the car of his wife's lover with concrete, and the ex-girlfriend who made a long-distance call from the ex-boyfriend's phone while he was on vacation, then left it off the hook. However, there is one tale of revenge that is true. In Sonnenberg, Germany, a mason going through a divorce chainsawed his single-story house in two, giving half of it to his ex-wife. The law was unhappy with his unique methods and punished him for the stunt. So while people consider and even go through with masterful revenge strategies, you are better off leaving the fantasies in your imagination.

Bargaining

"Maybe if I make varsity, he'll fall in love with me again."

"If she comes back to me, I'll stop hanging out with my friends three nights a week."

"If I had more money, would that change the way you feel about me?"

Welcome to the next stage of grieving. It is the sense that you can put off the inevitable or change it entirely — if only you could figure out what that one thing is that will make your ex change his or her mind. This is known as the **bargaining** stage, and as you stop being angry, you start to ask what you can do to make the other person take you back. In the traditional stages of grief, bargaining is talking to God or fate itself, to ask to live long enough to see a particular event happen. This represents a step forward, psychologically speaking. When someone reaches this stage while going through a breakup, psychologically he or she has accepted the relationship is over, even if he or she is trying to delay the breakup.

Bargaining with another person is different from bargaining with death. When trying to bargain in a relationship, you might hit on the right thing to say or do what will make the other person reconsider. Unlike bargaining with death, the other person is capable of changing his or her mind; maybe, you think, if you change the right thing about yourself, your ex will take you back. It does not hurt your chances that the person who broke up with you is feeling remorse of his or her own. However, one change will not put your relationship back together, or the breakup is only put off, not averted.

Depression

"I have lost her; I have lost everything. What is the point of life?"

"Why bother going to school or doing the laundry? It will not bring him back."

"What is the use? It does not work out."

After the fighting has been done and the bargains have been made, **depression** sets in. This is where the feelings of grief are finally processed and, unfortunately, it is not pretty. During bouts of depression, feelings of hopelessness, sadness and helplessness mix together. The person going through this stage might become withdrawn and introspective and spend time crying and mourning the loss of the relationship.

People coping with depression also do not feel like doing anything, which is why one of the common images of someone who has just gone through a breakup is the person on the couch, ice cream or video game controller in hand, watching the television for days.

How deeply people sink into depression after a breakup depends on several factors, including the length of the relationship, the depth of the relationship, and the amount of time spent together. Fortunately, this stage passes. Psychologists refer to this as slight depression, and the cure is time, getting some sleep, and support from family and friends. However, severe or clinical depression might occur as a result, and this can require psychiatric treatment. One in six teens suffers from depression, and while breaking up will not necessarily lead to severe depression, as a stressful event, it is a significant risk factor.

BROKEN HEART SYNDROME

Can you die of a broken heart? Believe it or not, there is such a thing as "broken heart syndrome."

Broken heart syndrome is referred to as stress cardiomyopathy. It is brought on by extreme and sudden emotional trauma. Although this can include undergoing a breakup, it is usually brought on by something more severe, such as experiencing the unexpected death of a loved one, being robbed at gunpoint, or being abused by a boyfriend or girlfriend. There are even some reports of broken heart syndrome being brought on by a surprise party.

The sufferers of this issue are usually postmenopausal women. The symptoms are similar to having a heart attack, and although heart failure is the same result for broken heart syndrome and a heart attack, they are not the same. Scientists have found that sufferers of broken heart syndrome have an odd type of weakness on the apex of the left ventricle of the heart. Although this might be an indicator of risk for the syndrome, there is no way to know for sure. Fortunately, if the sufferer can get to a hospital and receive care in time, he or she will survive and the weakness on the left ventricle will disappear. Experts theorize that broken heart syndrome is an unusual response to the chemicals the body generates during and after emotional trauma, such as adrenaline.

Acceptance

The final stage of grief is **acceptance**, when the grieving person realizes the loss has taken place, and he or she is at peace with the loss. He or she realizes that things will get better and that the loss, while painful, will not define him or her.

In the acceptance stage, a person will begin to live his or her life again. In terms of relationships, this means he or she might start dating again, or at least might be open to the possibility. He or she will also start to take responsibility and begin handling day-to-day tasks that he or she had ignored before while in the previous stages of grief. This is the most positive stage of the grieving process because it signifies the person is ready to move on with his or her life.

Acceptance should not be confused with a similar feeling — **resignation**. While actual acceptance entails understanding of the loss and being at peace with it, resignation is being submissive to the loss, even while harboring negative feelings. It is being constantly frustrated at the situation and feeling that there is no use in trying to fix it any more. This might lead to similar surface results as acceptance. The person appears calm, after all, and he or she is going about his or her normal routine as though nothing were wrong. After time has passed, though, friends and family might notice he or she does not put as much effort into living as he or she once did, or that he or she is more pessimistic than he or she was before the breakup. Acceptance is facing the situation as it is. Resignation is giving in.

Moving Through the Stages

At this point, you might be reading over the stages of grief and thinking, "I didn't deny anything. I just got depressed, then got angry, then got depressed again — what gives?"

No one reacts the same way to grief; Kübler-Ross mentioned that no one experiences the stages of grief in the same order, and people grieving will not experience every step of the model. However, a grieving person will experience at least two of the stages. More commonly, a person will hop from stage to stage and return to various stages multiple times before working through them. The important thing is that you will work through the process — at your own pace.

HOW TO BREAK UP IF A RELATIONSHIP TURNS VIOLENT

Get out. Period. If a relationship turns violent, the problem is not the lack of communication or the failure to address issues in the relationship. It is about not letting yourself be hurt. Although you might think you can work with your partner through this, the odds of a relationship becoming non-violent again with no outside help are low. Repeat domestic abuse in an abusive relationship is so common that it has its own cycle. It starts with the abuser harming the victim then feeling guilt over his or her actions. He or she then asks the victim to forgive him or her. If the victim grants it, the couple has a "honeymoon" period of reconciliation. The honeymoon lasts until the abuser becomes stressed again. After his or her stress level has built up enough, he or she takes it out on his or her partner by abusing him or her, which begins the cycle anew. Do not assume that just because the abuser feels guilty about his or her actions, the relationship will get better.

According to data Erin Marcus gathered in 2008, 10 women a day die from domestic violence in the United States, which totals 3,650 women a year. Every 12 seconds, a woman is beaten by her significant other. Need more incentive to leave an abusive relationship? In 2008, 511,000 women and 105,000 men were victims of domestic violence — enough people to fill a medium-sized city. Once a relationship turns violent, the time for talk is over, and the time for leaving is immediate. No matter what problems a relationship has, abuse is the ultimate deal-breaker. The National Coalition Against Domestic Violence advocates this sentiment, and you can learn more at its website at **www.ncadv.org**.

How to Cope Through the Stages of Grief

In a serious loss, such as a breakup, denial can manifest itself by your mind refusing to process the information. People report staring at the wall for hours on end as they try to come to grips with the fact that their relationship is over, or come to an understanding that they have suffered a serious loss, but letting their mind slide over what that loss is. This is known as shock, and it might take time for your mind to overcome it.

What is the best way to get over your denial? Acknowledge that your relationship is over. Then acknowledge that you feel hurt because of it. Your mind might want to stop thinking and go back into shock during this process. If it does, give it some time to recover, then acknowledge the loss again. Talking to yourself can do wonders here. Express how you feel, no matter how bad it is. Talk about whether you are angry or depressed, talk about how you feel toward your ex, and get everything out in the open with yourself. Only do this in your own home. If you share a room with siblings, wait until they are gone; this is something you must do for yourself, by yourself.

When confronting your denial, it is important not to fool yourself about the seriousness of the situation. You and your ex are not just going through a bad patch in your relationship; this is not a temporary separation. If you are aware that this breakup is permanent and you cannot bring it back, do not let yourself think otherwise. You will be doing yourself a favor if you just accept the grief instead of putting it off.

Introspection, devastation and flashes of emotion

After you overcome your disbelief of the situation and accept it, you are ready to face the next stage. This is a hard one to get through because this is where your feelings about the breakup make themselves known. These feelings can seem overpowering, and when you are in their grip, life can seem surreal. You feel disconnected from other people and tasks you are performing. The pain can be so strong that it takes a toll on your body. You feel so consumed with these feelings that getting out of bed takes an effort worthy of an Olympic athlete, and trying to take care of the day-to-day tasks of living now seems impossible.

Fortunately, these feelings do not last long. Instead, they come in bursts or spasms. When these bursts of grief hit you, they will not last forever. Narrow your focus down to getting through the rest of the hour, minute, or even second if you need to. Positive self-talk counts in this stage. Keep telling yourself you are going to get through this period, and everything will be better on the other end. This is not idle talk, either. You will feel better when you get through the current burst of grief, and you will feel better after you have passed through the anger and depression.

All in your head

During this period, you will also replay your relationship in your head as you are working through your heartbreak. Flashes of good times will be interspersed with the breakup scene, and thoughts of your ex as the person you fell in love with will come to mind. So will thoughts of your ex as he or she is now. It can be extremely frustrating to work with because during this time, you might feel you would be happier forgetting the relationship ever existed.

Despite how you are feeling about them, these flashes of memory are positive steps your mind is taking to process the breakup. Your romantic relationships can play a large role in your life, and relationships are built on memories and information. The only way you can let go of the relationship is for the mind to under-stand what the relationship was between you and your ex. This is an area where people feel compelled to talk to their ex about the relationship to get closure, but the truth is that you will have to come up with the answers yourself as your brain reviews the relationship in light of the breakup and comes to understand it and integrate it into your experience.

One of the best ways to cope with this is to keep a journal of what you are thinking and feeling. If one particular area of the relation-ship seems especially strong, write it in your journal and think about why it resonates so strongly with you. You will hear this advice throughout this book, but writing down the thoughts go-ing through your head solidifies them and makes them easier for your mind to understand. The more your mind can understand what is going on, the easier it will be able to process the information and the sooner you will get over your heartbreak.

Coping with anger

When you lose something you cherish, feeling angry is as natural as feeling depressed. This does not mean to act on your feelings. There are ways anger can manifest itself, none of which have a positive outcome. However, even though acting out your anger is bad, that does not mean not to confront it. Repressed anger comes through in other ways and makes a person mean-spirited and bitter. People who have repressed their anger might be constantly annoyed or prone to bad moods. When they interact with people, they might snap at them, delivering little below-the-radar insults that leave people feeling bad, even if they have no solid evidence that they were insulted.

To deal with your anger, the first thing you need to do is confront it. This anger is yours. Everything you are feeling as a result of this anger belongs to you. Acknowledging this might not be your proudest moment, but once you do, you can start to manage it. When you are aware you are angry, you can also understand who you are angry at, which is not the person in front of you who is not driving fast enough, the group of kids laughing and playing in the park, or the old lady in the express checkout lane with 64 cans of vegetables who is counting out the exact amount of change in pennies. Know whom you are getting angry at and why you are getting angry with them.

When you confront your anger, you might feel it is overwhelming you. You have energy, and you might want to take it out on someone. There are positive ways to channel that energy.

- Take any letters between you and your ex and rip them up. You might have to print out some of your ex's Facebook messages to rip them up, but it will feel satisfying when you do it.

- Make a punching bag or buy one from a sporting goods store. Hit it as hard as you can for as long as you can. A pillow is an acceptable substitute for a punching bag.

- Hit the gym or go swimming. Turn that energy into a trim, fit body.

- Talk with an understanding friend about how angry you are.

- Put on some music and sing along. Heavy metal bands work particularly well.

- Meditate. Take deep breaths and try to calm down.

If you feel that you might lose control when you express your anger, or if you feel that when you get angry you cannot hold it in, you might want to see an anger therapist. A place to start your search is at **www.4angertherapy.com.**

Dealing with depression

When you confront and manage your anger, you will find sadness on the other side. People in anger therapy, after having exhausted their rage supply, find that they start crying. One theory is that anger and sadness have the same core negative feeling. When it is turned on oneself, the result is depression. When it is turned on the rest of the world, it becomes anger.

Feeling depressed over the demise of a relationship is as natural as feeling anger. Human beings want to be loved, and when their feelings of love are rejected, they will normally feel depressed. If this is your first experience with heartbreak, you might feel alarmed at how intense your sadness can become. When you feel constantly tired or if you discover you cannot concentrate after a breakup, it is due to being depressed. Although feeling angry can give you excess energy, depression saps it from you. Feeling listless is common. So is feeling weak, which is all right because you might not have the motivation to do anything.

These periods of depression will pass. Although you are in the grip of them, you can still do things to lessen your pain. Take out your journal again and write down why you are feeling depressed. This will help organize your thoughts in the same way it does during the times when your mind starts thinking about your relationship and help you to understand your thoughts so you can work through them. Talking with friends is also a way to get through depression.

When you are coping with depression, surrounding yourself with positive thoughts can help. Focus on positive moments that happened during the day or during the week. Think about what you have accomplished, regardless of how small it is. You accomplished it in spite of being depressed. If there are any songs that make you feel better, give them a listen.

People can experience deep depression as a result of a breakup, or even become suicidal. This is not normal, and if you experience this, get help as soon as possible. Although you are aware of what feeling suicidal means, you might be less sure about the symptoms of deep depression. Feeling clinically depressed entails being so depressed you cannot function, and that there is no hope things will get better.

If you have not experienced this before, you might be puzzled about how you can tell whether you have hope, so here is a simple test. Look at yourself in the mirror and ask, "Are things going to get any better?" If you still have hope, you will be able to answer yes, no matter how much you qualify it. Even an answer like, "Things have to eventually get better" counts as a yes. If you do not have hope, on the other hand, even if you can bring yourself to say, "Yes," you will know you are lying. This is not an official psychological test, but it can be an indicator that you might want to visit a therapist.

If you feel suicidal, or if you feel that you are depressed beyond your capacity to function, go to an emergency room. If you feel that even contacting an emergency room is beyond your capacity, tell your family or friends and have them help you. Emergency rooms are equipped to handle psychological emergencies, and they will be able to provide you with some immediate care and call a therapist to determine the best course of action.

People refuse to get treatment for mental health issues, even if they suspect they might need it, because going to a psychologist is incorrectly perceived as a sign of weakness. While getting psychological help might not initially sound as noble or heroic as facing your problems yourself, the reality is that getting help when you need it is smart, not weak, and admitting you have a problem and facing up to reality takes more courage than being in denial about the situation. As movie director John Carpenter once said, "A strong man likes the feel of nature on his back, but a smart man knows when to get in out of the rain."

CASE STUDY: GETTING THROUGH THE GRIEF

Kara L.C. Jones had a different experience with heartbreak but experienced the same sense of grief and loss that one would in a breakup. She discusses how her journey through the grieving process has helped her to counsel others going through the same stages.

My own heartbreak came, not from a breakup, but from the death of my son on March 11, 1999. He died at birth after a full-term, perfectly healthy pregnancy. So to hear, "Your baby has no heartbeat," instead of, "It's a boy," was heartbreaking to say the least. In that first week after his death, the grief was too overwhelming to do much more than just feel miserable. Well-meaning friends and family were telling us things like, "You're young. You can try again." But the abyss between what I had wanted and what I now faced was just too big to be comforted by any such clichés. I found that creativity was my one safe haven. Making art was part of it, but it was also an everyday creativity. After all, it took creativity to find reasons why I should even bother getting out of bed each day after his death.

As time progressed and I had more energy, I got more adventurous in my creative explorations. Creative tools worked for me, such as art-making, writing in form, and guided visualization. Later, I began sharing my experiments with others in what became my Grief & Creativity Coaching practice. I found the techniques that worked for me as I had moved through the heartbreak of our son's death were the same techniques that worked for clients dealing with relationship breakups.

Here are some techniques clients have said were helpful to them during breakups:

1) Facing the abyss between what was wanted and what is now. We do guided visualizations together to see and feel ourselves standing at the edge of what we had wanted. We allow ourselves to face this abyss of loss and look for the bridges that might let us cross to a more peaceful space, remembering our broken hearts. Some clients find it helpful to journal or do collage work afterward to explore the visualizations.

2) Practicing permission. We look at where we are stopping ourselves. We ask ourselves honestly where we are not granting ourselves permission. And then we create permission slips for ourselves to allow for practicing how to do and feel whatever we need to do and feel. Examples: "I have permission to just be in my funk and see what is there," "I have permission to grieve in more than five stages," or "I have permission to celebrate the holiday and feel icky at the same time."

It allows us to make visible what might otherwise be invisible, tucked away inside, as we put on our masks to try and get back to work or do the things demanded of us in our everyday lives.

3) Letting our experiences transform to get a different perspective. For this one, you pick some element of nature that represents your experience, such as a storm. Then you list all the attributes of a storm: windy, dark, cold, unpredictable and damaging. And then you journal about your experience using those attributes — the idea being that you get a look at your experience in a different light or as something more outside yourself. Here is an example using "gale-force winds" as the element:

Gale Force, by Kara L.C. Jones

I used to be a gale, soaring into any room with an outburst of laughter, a pouring of sunny miracles. But since my son died, I am a sallow fog, a damp veil hanging from thin air with the ability to unsettle the marrow from your bones. Birds don't like my moist tears on their wings, but some — like the black birds — gather to crow dirges, giving voice to sorrow over the lands. I used to be a gale who would just breeze by. Now I am a mist, a permanent part of your land.

Some clients like to write in journal style, while others might write in poetic format. Other clients like to take the element of nature they choose and cut out images from old magazines that illustrate the attributes. Then they will make collage art exploring the "storm of grief" or whatever they are experiencing in the moment.

None of this is about finding *the answers*. It is about showing up consciously for whatever you are feeling and allowing those feelings to be expressed. It is about expressing your experience in a different way so that you might glimpse a different perspective and shift your process. Each small expression experiment helped me in some way to begin understanding an otherwise overwhelming heartbreak. Creativity, in forms and formats, was my heartbreak salve.

Anxiety and guilt

Two close cousins of depression are anxiety and guilt. Neither is pleasant.

When anxiety hits, such as when you see your ex unexpectedly, you might mistake it for restlessness, at least until it increases. When it becomes worse, anxiety feels as though your body is on red alert against an unknown threat. Your hands might shake, your heart might feel like it has gotten a dose of adrenaline, and you will notice every movement and noise. At higher levels, anxiety can cause you to lose sleep or be unable to eat. Although these problems can be solved with medication, you might want to practice some techniques to help you relax.

Pick a room, such as your den or bedroom, to serve as your relaxation room. Buy some candles for it, and make sure you can adjust the blinds to make the lighting more subdued. Get some calming music, or buy a CD full of white noise, such as rainstorm or beach sounds. Then lie down and try to picture yourself somewhere else. Lie there until you feel calm again, and repeat this technique. You might also want to add some of your own touches to this room, such as scented candles or incense. The more relaxed you become, the less anxiety will affect you.

Guilt, on the other hand, has no physical symptoms. In relationships, both sides will feel guilty it ended. If you broke up with your partner, you might feel guilty that you did not try harder to save the relationship. If you have been broken up with, you might feel guilty that you did not do enough in the relationship to make your partner happy with it. At this point, you might feel you can come up with a dozen things you could have done better in your relationship without having to think hard.

What is especially insidious about guilt is that it leads you to think you still have some control over the breakup. Because the dissolution of the relationship was your fault, that must mean you can apologize and make things better again, right?

But the problem is that even if you apologize, you cannot change the past. If you did not commit one of the unforgivable sins of a relationship, such as cheating on or abusing your partner, then you did not do any one thing to cause the relationship to fail.

Even if you can come up with some definite ways you were a bad boyfriend or girlfriend, you cannot beat yourself up over them. It is unproductive at best and, at worst, the guilt will prevent you from being in another romantic relationship for a long time, until you learn to forgive yourself. While you cannot move on if you believe you can apologize and save your relationship, you also cannot move on if you keep beating yourself up.

If you want to impress your ex, take responsibility for the mistakes you made, then put those lessons to use in your next relationship. If you and your ex ever meet again, he or she will be impressed with how you have changed. Take out your journal and write about your guilty feelings in there. Discuss how you can put those lessons to use in your next relationship. If you still feel guilty, you can write a letter of apology to your ex. Write down everything you would like to say to him or her, then seal it in an envelope or save it to your computer. Avoid mailing it until after you are over your ex.

None of the above

At some point, all these intense emotions you have been feeling will collide and, in the grand tradition of equal and opposite forces everywhere, cancel each other out and leave you in a state of **ambivalence**, or uncertainty about how to feel. You might feel calm, somewhat at peace, and perhaps even indifferent to your breakup during this state. Although this might be a relief, as you are now free from these intense negative emotions that have been threatening to consume you, feeling ambivalent can also be confusing. The sensation of feeling nothing when you feel you should be feeling something can be disturbing, and you might wonder what is wrong with you.

Unlike other emotional states during the grieving process, this is one for which to feel thankful. Appreciate the calmness your mind is giving you, and take this moment to relax. The other feelings will be back, and you will continue on the grieving process. Allow yourself the time to feel other emotions, then work with the anger and sadness.

Accepting and moving on

The final stage, **acceptance**, is something to welcome, not cope with. You might not realize you are in the acceptance stage until after the fact, such as when you drive to school and realize you have not thought about your ex for a week. Acceptance begins with brief periods of being at peace with yourself among the feelings of depression and anger. In time, these periods grow longer, and the periods of depression and anger become shorter.

The acceptance period brings with it a new understanding of what life is about. There might not be just one right answer to what life is about, but at this point, you have found the answer that works for you. This newfound clarity results in people going through their life and reevaluating it — a spiritual spring cleaning. During this time, people might make major changes based on their newfound clarity. They might decide to become serious about things they have dreamed of doing, they might decide to join a new club or organization, or maybe they will pick up a new hobby.

When you are in the middle of this phase, enjoy it. You have earned the right after what you have been through in the wake of your breakup. Consider the goals you want to achieve with your new understanding, and use the courage and strength you have acquired as a result of this process to their best advantage.

Now it is time to start discussing areas of the breakup in depth. What is the best way to cope with seeing your ex again? What do you do for fun now that your ex is not around? Where do you go from here? The answers are just ahead.

CASE STUDY:
MOVING THROUGH
THE GRIEVING PROCESS

Faydra Rector is a certified life coach with a Master of Arts in psychology and more than 14 years of experience in the field of relationships. She wrote a weekly newspaper column called "Life Coach" for the Red Bluff Daily News and has been featured in multiple podcasts.

Here is her advice on coping with breakups.

The biggest problem I see people trying to overcome is allowing themselves to go through the cycle of grief, as shown by this chart:

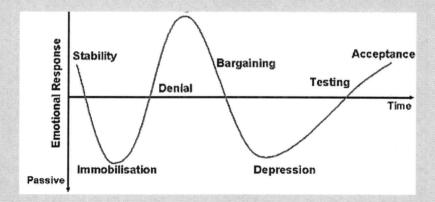

Any loss falls into the grief cycle. A breakup is no different. My clients get stuck in one phase of grief and sit there for years. For example, there are people who become so angry at their ex or the circumstances that surround the breakup that they take that anger with them into any new relationship. They, in essence, could not make their partner pay, so they transfer that "balance due" to everyone else. Once I help them see they have taken this baggage with them, they are horrified to see what they have done.

Another way that they stay stuck is by refusing to accept or let go of the situation. People tend to romanticize their relationships when they are over-analyzing the issues that led to the breakup. This can keep them in the denial or bargaining phase of the grief cycle. I try to help people see that there are legitimate issues when a relationship does not work out. The sooner people acknowledge that they need to say goodbye to what they had, the sooner they can heal and find the life they desire.

The depression phase of the relationship grief cycle can keep people from making personal choices that will move them closer to healing. People eat too much or too little, exercise too much, or let it all go. The sense of the relationship being all they will ever have becomes a bigger loss issue than the hope of finding a new and better life. Age and economics also play a huge role in this.

In my divorce-coaching practice, one of the first things I work on with people is educating them about their own issues as they relate to their exes. People have deep-seated issues with their ex or else they would not be getting separated. I coach people to realize that they can only control three things in their life: their thoughts, feelings and actions. They cannot control another person in any way. They might be able to manipulate them, push their buttons, or make them have a hard time, but they cannot control them. Likewise, their exes can push their buttons, make life hard, and do mean things, but they cannot control their responses. People train one another how to treat them. As Eleanor Roosevelt said, "No one can make you feel inferior without your consent."

When speaking about your ex, limit your comments to the old saying: If you can't say something nice, don't say anything.

Sometimes the issues that surrounded your breakup can be likened to an addiction. If you are trying to stop being a cheater, you should not go and flirt with people. The same is true with your relationship. If you always went to the same place for dinner on Saturday night and sat in the corner booth and shared a milkshake, do not go to that place, *ever*.

Do not look at old pictures and romanticize the situation. Likewise, do not look at old pictures and seethe about what a jerk they were. Close Facebook and get rid of the things that make you stay stuck in the grief cycle.

Additionally, train yourself to speak in the present. Your friends want to support you and love you through your mess; make sure you don't spend your time with them talking incessantly about your ex, your drama and your pain. What you think about and speak about is what you bring about. If all you do is talk about your pain, you leave little room for a new life to seep in.

Chapter 3

The Disengagement Protocols

Now that you have an understanding of how relationships fall apart and what the grieving process is like, you are ready to take on your broken heart. So, what is the first step on the road to recovery? It is simple — do not call. Do not text. Do not DM.

Now that your relationship has ended, you desperately need to talk to someone — someone who knows you, someone who understands you, and someone whom you can count on to make you feel better. Unfortunately, the first person you might think of is your ex. This is the kind of no-win situation that has inspired people to find the nearest convenient wall against which they can pound their heads.

Then again, maybe you do not want your ex to comfort you. Maybe you are doing just fine without her, except you just got the car washed and cleaned, and she complained about that. What could possibly make her happier than calling her up and telling her that one of her biggest pet peeves is no longer a problem? Also, if you call her, you can show her that you are not the same person you were before. You have changed, and you are the kind of person that she wants to spend time with, or maybe even fall in love with. Now, if you could just find the right words to say it.

Do you see the trap? The one person in the world you want to communicate with is the one person with whom you need to cut off all forms of communication. But if you keep talking to your ex, you will not be able to cut the emotional ties with him or her and move on. According to grief counselor Dr. Susan J. Elliott, the one problem common to everyone who struggles through a breakup is that, for whatever reason, they just cannot or do not want to stop communicating with their exes. Even after it is clear the relationship is well and over, people still have trouble shutting off all forms of communication. But if you are ever going to get the space you need to emotionally heal and come to peace with the loss of your relationship, it is a step you must take.

The problem in the 21st century is that communicating is easy. While you can pick up your cellphone and easily give your ex a call or shoot him a quick text, you can also check his social media sites or contact him through direct messaging. He can also contact you.

What is the best solution to this problem? You are going to need to steel your resolve. Take a moment and calm yourself. Do whatever you need to do to get yourself in the frame of mind to make a big decision. When you are ready, make a commitment to yourself that you are not going to contact him or her again, in any way, shape, or form. Ideally, do not set any sort of time limit on this communications blackout, but at least maintain it for a month or two.

When you begin your period of no communication with your ex, though, you might want to let her know about it, especially if you communicate on a social media site. Write her a brief message and say that due to the breakup, you need to spend time away from her before you can figure out where the two of you stand. Send it to her and then get rid of your ex's contact information. Delete her number from your cellphone, go to your email and delete her email address, then unfollow or delete her as a friend on any social media pages.

While you can hide your status and updates from your ex, if you do not unfollow him, you will be able to see what he is doing, unless he hides his status and updates or unfollows you first. Also, change the relationship status of your social media pages to "single." Do not put this off. The longer you wait to do it, the longer you will be reminded that you were in a relationship with your ex. Setting your social media relationship status to single is like pulling off a bandage quickly. It will hurt at first, but you can start recovering from the pain that much sooner.

Delete him or her from your address book and contact lists, written and digital. If you feel you must keep his or her contact information, write it on an index card. But once you do, put the card out of sight in an area you will not be able to reach easily. Better yet, give the card to a friend and ask him or her to store it in a safe place. Tell him or her not to give it back to you until at least a month has passed.

Once you have that taken care of, the hard part begins. At this point, the void the other person has left is going to make itself known. Whom are you going to talk to now that the person who knew you better than anyone else is gone? What should you do with yourself when the only thing you want to do is call him or her up and just to hear a quick "Hello?" The good news is that the emptiness created by completely cutting yourself off from your ex eventually disappears. Breaking up with your ex is like overcoming a drug addiction in ways, and to a certain extent, you are psychologically addicted to your ex's company. You need to go through the withdrawal stage to feel better. How long does this take? It depends on the person. People have trouble for a day or two before they realize they are feeling better. Some people might have to wait a while. Others might have to wait even longer.

Fortunately, you will not be alone when you decide to stop having contact with your ex. Contact your family and your friends, and get a sense of times they are available to talk. Let them know you are trying not to talk to your ex, and ask if you could talk to them instead. For your benefit and theirs, make a schedule of when they are available, and make sure you do not rely on one person. When you feel you need to contact your ex, contact one of the people from your list instead.

Throughout the day, make sure you take care of yourself. Falling back into a bad habit is easier if you are physically or mentally exhausted. Get exercise daily to avoid feeling rundown, and if you can, avoid running yourself ragged while at school. Make sure to not skip meals, and get at least eight hours of sleep. Just as important is to do some nice things for yourself. Eat out with friends, or buy that book you have been curious about reading.

That being said, you might still feel the need to contact your ex. If you do, you can take a lesson from people who are going through behavioral therapy for compulsive behaviors, such as overeating — keep a journal. Buy a small notebook, and keep it in easy reach of your computer or phone. The next time you want to contact your ex, or the next time you break down and talk to your ex, get out the journal and write about your state of mind when you called him or her. Write about what you were feeling, what you were thinking, and what you wanted to say. Then, start asking questions. Examine your feelings and ask yourself about why you want to stay in contact. Here are some sample questions to get you started:

- What did I hope to get out of this conversation?

- What do I want to take away from this conversation?

- What do I want my ex to take away from this conversation?

- How do I want to feel after the conversation is done?

- How do I want my ex to feel after the conversation?

- How was I feeling when I decided I wanted to talk to my ex?

- Would you rather receive bad attention from your ex than none?

As you keep track of your emotions, you will be able to realize exactly why you want to contact your ex. After that, you can plan what you will do the next time you feel the urge to call, write, or text. For example, after keeping a journal for a week, you might realize that you get the urge to call your ex after watching the food channel because you liked to cook dinner for your ex, who was appreciative when you did. From there, you can formulate a list of things you can do to stave off the urge. A good plan based on this example is:

CHECKLIST:

♡ First, select a friend who also has an interest in cooking. Talk with him or her and explain how watching the food channel makes you nostalgic for the time you spent with your ex.

♡ Second, go for a walk.

♡ Third, write about how you are feeling. Go back to your journal and pour your heart out.

♡ Fourth, go to the gym.

♡ Fifth, cook. Why not let that television episode inspire you? Try out a recipe you have been thinking of, or make an old favorite. Get involved in your hobby and feel happy that you are doing it for yourself. The fact that you can taste the fruits of your labors is an added bonus.

♡ Last, take a shower.

Creating Your Own Plan

"Anyone with a broken heart who enjoys cooking is taken care of, but what about people like me, who like rock climbing? What about all the rest of us?" The answer is that creating a plan to avoid contact with your ex does not just depend on your hobby. It is a personal process, and you will likely be refining it from day to day.

To start making a plan, get a sheet of paper and read through your journal about all the times you have wanted to call your ex. As you read through your journal, come up with activities that can take your mind off how you feel. Some samples are listed below:

- **Take a shower.** While you might also consider taking a bath, taking a shower is more active because you are washing yourself, washing your hair, and perhaps even shaving while you are standing up. It is more engaging than taking a bath, it will occupy your mind with thoughts other than calling your ex, and as hundreds of movies and romantic novels have shown, it is a way to relieve stress.

- **Exercise.** Burn off extra emotional energy. Plus, exercising raises your serotonin levels, makes you feel better and combats the negative emotions you are feeling.

- **Go for a walk.** Walking is simple activity you can do anywhere, and it will give you time to calm down so your emotions are not in charge anymore.

- **Visit your local mall.** Although buying things is only a temporary fix for unhappiness, activities such as window-shopping do not have to include buying anything. This is another activity that will make you feel better and draw attention away from contacting your ex.

- **Visit your neighborhood park.** People like to be in the city, while others enjoy the feel of nature around them. Spending time in your local park is a way to restore your peace of mind, and parks have free-to-use facilities for activities, such as tennis courts, basketball hoops, or disc golf courses.

- **Write in your journal.** The journal does not just have to be for chronicling when you want to call your ex. Pour out your heart. Write down everything about how you feel, your state of mind, and try to put into words just why it is that your ex is the only person you need to talk to at this moment. One of the nice things about writing your thoughts down is that you are forced to clarify what you are thinking, and when you are able to go back and read what you have written, you can think about your feelings with a level head.

- **Work on a hobby or craft.** This is another way to regain your peace of mind. Also, hobbies, from playing video games to photography, will give you time to calm down and think about why you want to contact your ex, and why doing so might not be as good an idea as you initially thought. Plus, when you work on a hobby, you are concentrating on your needs, not the needs of your relationship.

- **Do housekeeping.** It might not be as fun as doing a favorite hobby, exercising, or talking to a friend or family member, but if you make a commitment to yourself that you need to do your laundry or vacuum your bedroom before calling, you will prevent the stereotypical "messy house" syndrome that is a staple of movie and television breakups and will have another way to give yourself a cool-down period, the same way you would as a hobby. Housekeeping is also like a hobby because you are doing something for yourself.

- **Do homework.** This is similar to doing housework because it is less fun than going to the mall, working on a hobby, or talking with a friend. On the other hand, it is something that you need to do anyway, and as you take your mind off your ex, you are doing something for yourself.

Once you come up with a list of activities, pick five or six you think will take your mind off wanting to contact your ex. Make a list, and post it by your telephone. Given that people use their cellphones as their main phone line, a good alternative might be to place your list by your computer to avoid messaging your ex. The next time you feel the need to contact your ex, go to your list and do the first activity. After you are done with the first activity, if the urge to contact your ex has passed, you can smile and go about your day. If it has not, go to the list again and do the next item. Repeat until you no longer have the urge to contact your ex.

If you end up calling your ex in spite of this list, do not beat yourself up. Go back to your journal and answer the same questions you asked when you came up with your plan. Then think about how the activities you listed did not help you out of your mental state and revise your list accordingly.

Did you just feel you could not help yourself with the phone and computer in easy reach? Next time leave your cellphone in a different room from whatever activity you are doing. Was your hobby the strongest tie you had with your ex? Switch out doing your hobby with another activity. Keep revising this list until you find the activities that work for you. But make sure that they are things you want to do. You might ask other people for their advice on creating this list, but you have the final say in what will heal you. So your friend thinks you should invest some serious money into a bicycle and go out cycling? So your mother says that this is the perfect time to get a membership to the gym and drop those 20 pounds she has been nagging you about for the past year? Figure out if they will help you. If you do not see the appeal in cycling, or you do not want to have to deal with the pressure of trying to lose weight on top of dealing with your breakup, then feel free to lose that suggestion in favor of an activity that works for you.

CASE STUDY:
A COUNSELOR WHO HAS
BEEN IN THE TRENCHES

If there is one person who should stand as a beacon of light at the end of the breakup tunnel, it is Ken Donaldson. He has overcome divorce, depression and addiction to be a psychotherapist, author, speaker and relationship coach. He is one of six recipients who won the 2006 Tampa Bay Health Care Hero Award, and he is the founder of the Personal Empowerment Coaching Program. Here he shares some advice on getting through your breakup.

"Getting through the pain is the biggest challenge," Ken says, "plain and simple. It feels like it's going to last forever. Or that you're forever scarred. Minutes seem like weeks and days seem like years. And then there's also all the racing thoughts: 'Why did this happen?' and 'What did I do wrong?' are common, but the [biggest one] is, 'Why does this happen to me?'"

As you work on healing yourself, you need to give yourself time, "as much as you need," according to Ken. "Talk about it with your friends if you need to, and write about it if that helps. But more than anything else, just give it time. Time does heal all wounds, especially if it is guilt-free, shame-free and resentment-free."

Healing from a broken heart is a different process for everyone, according to Ken. However, he has advice for those going through breakups. "Use your support system and surround yourself with compassionate and understanding people," he says. "Realize, however, that some people don't know what to do or say, so they do or say things that can be counterproductive. Joining a support group or therapy group can also be beneficial." Ken also cautions against hanging around people who are too zealous in taking your side. "Don't allow the negative people to bombard you with conversation about how bad [your ex] was."

Ken also encourages harnessing your artistic side during the breakup. "Music, dance and artwork are all forms of self-expression that can be helpful in the healing process," he says.

However, Ken also warns against three behaviors that can impede the healing process. "If you immediately start dating again," he says, "you'll likely carry all the hurt, anger and whatever else you're feeling right into the next relationship. Also, your thinking and 'picking mechanism' is not going to be grounded and clear during this time, so you're likely to get into something that could be highly dysfunctional."

The second behavior to avoid is playing the blame game. "It's easy to take the other person's inventory and look at everything they did wrong or bad, even if they did do inappropriate things," Ken says. "But what's the point? The more time and energy you spend focused on that, the longer it'll take you to move on."

Finally, do not fall into the mentality of being the victim. "How about this: It's no one's fault. It just happened. Period," Ken suggests. "Even though it might not make sense and even though there might be unanswered questions, this is the time to heal and begin to move forward. Instead of getting into, 'Why does this happen to me?' or 'I can't believe he/she did this to me,' how about, 'Live and let live'? Just pay attention to what you need right now. This also includes getting into lengthy discussions with your friends about how bad [your ex] was. It's time to release and mend your own heart. Staying focused on the pain will only keep you focused on the pain."

When the topic shifts to whether to see your ex again, Ken is reluctant to give a hard and fast answer. "It all depends on a number of dynamics," he explains. "If seeing your ex only makes you feel worse, then no. If the two of you fight or argue — maybe just like the old days — then no again. But if the two of you can have a good conversation, or better yet, a healing conversation, then sure, go ahead and see each other. Can the two of you celebrate the wonderful times you spent together? Can you tell each other what you appreciate about each other? Can you, in a loving way, also share with each other what didn't work or what was unacceptable? Perhaps you can even kindle a friendship from this. Give this all the time it needs, and don't try to rush it. This might be a vulnerable time and you might not be seeing things clearly if there is still emotion going on."

Since everyone heals at an individual rate, there is not a defined timetable for when you feel up to dating again. However, Ken urges people who have suffered a breakup to not rush things. "Better to go slow than fast, as a rule," he says. "People dive into another relationship as a way to avoid the pain from the former one and only make things worse for themselves. When you do start to date again, go slow. Ask questions and remember what you learned from your past relationship. Perhaps your last relationship opened some insights to yourself, things you didn't know about yourself previously. Play those new insights forward and create new boundaries for yourself. Be cautious and keep shuffling your feet forward."

When you finally do go on a date, Ken urges people to be patient. "Remember what you've learned. Think from your head, not your heart, meaning you need to make sure that you're clear about your deal-makers and deal-breakers and that you stick to your boundaries and limits. If you're not sure about all this, then it's time to get clear. Use your support system to help, or maybe even a counselor if you can't figure this out for yourself."

One of the best traits that can get you through a breakup is decisiveness, according to Ken. "Decide that [your relationship] is done if it's truly done and begin to heal, recover and move on. People go back and forth unnecessarily, causing more pain. If you haven't done everything possible, then perhaps you'll want to get a counselor involved, but at some point you have to decide to either repair the relationship or move on. Limbo-land will drain the life out of you."

Excuses, Excuses

Another problem that comes up when trying to cut off contact with one's ex is that people can think of reasons why they need to be in touch. There might be something they are looking for their exes to give them, or perhaps they are looking to have that one conversation that will wrap up the relationship so they can continue. Grief counselor Dr. Susan Elliott has found that when someone wants to see his or her ex again, he or she will come up with one of seven different reasons why he or she should contact him or her. There will be an infinite number of variations on these excuses, but with a little questioning about the person's reasons, one of these excuses will show up.

Closure

The first excuse is getting **closure**, when you have to know what happened to your relationship. If you just knew what went wrong in this relationship, you would be able to close the book on this chapter in your life and move on, free of pain and guilt. The only way you feel you will ever get closure is to talk with your ex and understand how and why this happened.

Getting closure is something people want in their relationships, but thinking it can only be reached after hashing out your relationship with your ex is a mistake. You might have questions about what went wrong, and these questions might bother you. However, talking with your ex about these questions does not give you the answers you are looking for. The answers he or she gives you might make sense initially, at least until you start thinking about them. If he or she says, "We could not agree on when to go out and with who," you might be satisfied for a day or so, until you start thinking of the times that you did agree on hanging out with a specific friend group and there will be exceptions to reasons your ex gives. This leads to the conclusion that there must have been a deeper reason, and you need to call your ex again to ask about it. If you happen to be reading this and wincing at the familiarity, do not be too hard on yourself. People have fallen into the trap of thinking that their ex's answers are unsatisfying and that there has to be an even deeper reason behind their breakup.

You also run the risk that the closure you get will make you feel worse. What if your ex sends you one email then refuses to respond to your other questions? What if he or she simply ignores your request for closure entirely? Worse yet, your ex might use this opportunity to harass you and list all your faults in alphabetical order or deliver insult after insult about everything relating to you while implying that you need to lower your standards.

Either way, you will have to accept the fact that your ex cannot give you the answers that will give you closure. The closure you seek has to come from within. Also, a large part of that closure will be accepting the fact that life does not give you answers, not even to questions you feel are important. Instead, you need to accept that the experience happened, learn to draw from its lessons, and move on. It is not easy, and there is no one way to do it.

Just one more thing to say

Tied close with the concept of closure is the excuse of saying one last thing. While you might have been questioning your ex about why things went wrong in the relationship, the belief that you need to say one last thing is understandable, especially if you were the one dumped. Again, it is another common cliché in countless love-themed novels and romantic comedies. If you just make one touching display of your love, or say the right thing, your lover will come running back to your arms and not get on that plane to Paris or New Jersey. So, you think to yourself, is there any reason this cannot be your moment?

Unfortunately, there are reasons why this cannot work. The biggest one is that relationships do not just suddenly come into being. Similarly, relationships do not just fall apart overnight. Your relationship might have dissolved when you caught your significant other with someone else, but there was a long, slow road to that point. Either that, or he or she did not intend to be faithful to you. Regardless of the reason, you cannot change your partner's mind over the course of just one conversation. At the least, it would take weeks of talking and convincing to make your partner think the two of you should get back together, and that is only if they are open to the possibility in the first place. Otherwise, you are crossing the fine line from "impassioned" to "stalker," and that can create problems larger than a broken heart. The bottom line is that you two are different people, and as things stand, neither of you are compatible. It is a harsh truth to admit, but the sooner you admit it, the sooner you can start moving on.

Another reason behind saying one last thing is to prove your ex wrong about his view of you. You just need to tell him that you are mature, that you are responsible, and that you respect his boundaries before you move on with your life. This is similar to closure, but in this instance you need your ex to deny his criticisms of you before you can start dating. Given that trying to change his mind is going to erupt into an argument before you hang up, he is unlikely to take back his assessment of you. In terms of an excuse to contact your ex, this is something of a sustaining cycle where you contact him, fail to change his mind, then contact him later, when you are determined to change his mind — and he is equally determined that you will not.

If you are upset at something your ex said to you during the breakup process, the person whose opinion you need to adjust is yours. Why should his or her opinion of you, especially at a point where negative emotions are running high, matter? Is his or her opinion of you more important than yours? The best thing you can do is repeat, "Who cares what he or she thinks?" If there is one person in this world who should not have to care what your ex thinks, it is you.

MAILING YOUR BREAKUP IN

If you want to contact your ex about something he or she said that hurt you, use the old behavioral therapy method of writing a letter.

The process is simple: When you feel you need to contact your ex about an issue, instead of picking up the telephone or going to your email account, take out a sheet of paper and start writing instead.

Discuss each issue and take as much time as you need to express yourself. Be as emotional as you would like. Then, fold the letter and put it in an envelope. Last, do not send the letter.

Instead, burn it, shred it, or find another way to make sure no one else will read what you have written. This letter is not meant for your ex; it is meant to help you solidify your thoughts about your ex, and writing your thoughts down is an excellent way to express your feelings without running the risk of any hard feelings resulting from sharing them.

Writing down your thoughts can also make you aware of the issues you have regarding your ex. And once you know what those issues are, you will have an easier time sorting them out

If you do not have a pencil or pen and paper, you can turn to the 21st -century equivalent — your computer's word processor. The process is the same, with the exception that you should empty your computer's recycling or garbage bin after deleting the document.

Have to get my stuff back

As far as excuses go, the "returning stuff" reasoning is a thinly disguised excuse to see your ex again. It can also be used to fool yourself. While you might know not to try to get closure or get the last word in, you might realize that your ex still has your favorite sweater. So what choice do you have but to visit him or her — even though you do not want to, and you know that it would be better for all concerned if you did not go there?

If you do want your stuff back from a breakup, you and your ex should agree to do a mutual return within days of the event. The longer you wait, the less justification you will have for trying to get your things back. Also after "a reasonable time" (weeks), your ex can legally assume custody of your stuff and do with it as he or she sees fit, although it is a blurry area, legally. If you need a good reason to get your stuff back quickly after the breakup, this is it. If you still have things that belong to your ex, or you want some things back from your ex, take time and get all the items you want to return into one pile. Make a list of all the things you want back from your ex. Then contact him or her, make the trade, and do not contact him or her again.

While on the subject of getting stuff back, do not try to get gifts back. They belong to your ex now.

I still want to be friends

As opposed to other excuses, the "let's be friends" reason for keeping in contact might seem like the best way to show you are moving on with your life while still keeping in contact with your ex, making the breakup hurt less. At least, that is the theory. In reality, being friends with your ex after breaking up will drag you into the same problems of contacting your ex that bother those who rely on other excuses. The problem is that you and your ex still need to explore the ruins of your relationship and come to a sense of closure about it. Part of that closure is going to involve getting over your feelings for your ex, and you will not be able to do that if you are still in contact with him or her. You are going to need some time to reestablish yourself as a single person and not part of a couple.

Trying to be friends with your ex is also problematic because of all the history you have with him or her. You can joke around and tease your friends, but with your ex, all the things that make a friendship suddenly become a minefield. Unless you and your ex are formal and polite all the time, the odds are high that one of you will say something that touches on a sore spot in your relationship. It is one thing to tease a friend about how messy his room is; it is another to tease your ex about a messy room, especially if that was one of the problems you had with him.

Unlike the other excuses, though, being friends with your ex after you have broken up is achievable. It just should not be attempted immediately after you have broken up with him or her. Let the bonds between you and your ex dissolve until you start thinking of the two of you as separate entities, as opposed to still being a couple. This is going to take time, and ideally, during that time you will be free of your ex. There is no one-size-fits-all time limit here, but a good rule of thumb is at least a year. People might need more time than that. So at the end of a year, ask yourself honestly if you want to see your ex again to show him or her how much you have grown as a person and how you are now, or if you miss the non-relationship stuff you did. You want to see him or her as a person, complete with his or her strengths and flaws, then evaluate if you want to let him or her in your life again.

Being friends with your ex after breaking up differs from the other types of excuses because it has a negative aspect that is different from wanting to get back with your ex. According to Dr. Elliot, people push to remain friends with their ex because they want to keep the companionship the other person provided without having to deal with the bad parts of the relationship, such as the responsibility or commitment.

If you insist that your ex should remain in touch with you to preserve the friendship, you need to examine your motivations. Do you think you can stand seeing your ex as a friend, even when he or she starts dating someone else? Are you trying to avoid the negative feelings that inevitably accompany a breakup? Even though you wanted to end the relationship, do you still want to keep ties to him or her? Are you trying to get all the positives of the relationship without any of the negatives?

On the other side, if your ex asks you to be a friend, consider whether this will be beneficial for you. Do you think your ex will value you as a friend the same way your other friends do?

What do you get out of your friendships, and will your ex provide it? Do you think you can stand to see your ex date someone else and then brag to you, as his or her friend, about how well his or her date went?

If your ex wants you two to be friends, you have the right to say no. Your ex might in response tell you that you need to grow up, or that you are not being fair. If he or she says any of these things to you, feel free to ignore him or her. Being friends with someone should not rely on one person pressuring another into friendship. Both sides need to agree to be friends. One person deciding for the other is not a friendship.

Just in case they want to get back together

Other times, people want to keep in contact with their ex to be available to get back together. The line of thinking is that if you cut off all forms of communication with your ex, you run the risk of not being available if he or she decides the breakup was a mistake. How bad would you feel if he or she calls you, gets your voice mail, and decides that because you did not answer the call, you do not want to get back together?

This excuse works together with several others. You might want to be friends because you need to show him or her who you are, which will make him or her want to reconcile with you, and you need to be available for that. Or you might need to say one last thing that will completely change his or her mind about you, and when that does happen, you will need to be available when he or she decides to reconcile.

The nice thing about this excuse is how quickly it evaporates if you think about it. If your ex contacts you once or twice and decides not to reconcile with you, then he or she must not have been that serious about it. Think about what you would do if you wanted to reconcile with your ex: Do you think you would give up after a call or text went unanswered? If your ex wants to reconcile with you, he or she will get the message to you somehow.

In addition, the fact that you will not be able to move on if you keep talking to your ex needs to be repeated. If there is going to be any hope of reconciliation, it will not be during the 56th time you have contacted him or her to see if he or she is ready to reconcile with you.

We cannot avoid seeing each other

The final reason couples have for seeing each other outside the breakup is that they have to see each other. Perhaps you go to school together. Perhaps you have the same hobbies and the same circle of friends, or you work together. Either way, for some reason, you cannot cut off all contact with him or her.

You win this one. You cannot realistically cut off all contact with your ex in this situation. However, you can still seek to minimize contact with your ex. If you know you are going to be seeing him or her ahead of time, then set up some ground rules. Make some guidelines about what will and will not be discussed. For instance, if you are in the same class, agree that you will only talk about school matters with him or her. If your ex refuses to discuss this with you, then you have to set up the guidelines yourself. You will not be able to control what your ex wants to say, but you can limit yourself. If your ex brings up a topic that you would rather not discuss, let him or her know. Be polite about it, but do not back down.

The same rules apply if you have the same hobbies. Do not actively avoid your ex, though. If your ex greets you, greet him or her back. If your ex asks how you are, you can tell him or her you are doing well. After that, you can politely excuse yourself.

TIME TO LEAVE

In certain situations, staying in your social circle might not be the best option. Perhaps your ex has gotten over you before you have done the same. Maybe you feel your ex is trying to lure you into fighting with him or her. Maybe your ex arrives with a new boyfriend or girlfriend, or constantly brings in new boyfriends or girlfriends. In these situations, you might want to consider taking some time off from your group. If you are thinking to yourself that having to leave your social circle is not fair, you are correct. It is not fair, and it is not right. However, if your options are between leaving your social circle or being hurt on a regular basis, taking some time off from your circle of friends might be your best choice.

Before you leave, plan what you are going to do. Ask your friends if there are any groups in the area with similar interests to yours. Talk with any friends you have in other social circles and deepen your connections with them.

Make some plans so you do not spend your weekends trapped at home trying to finish a marathon of television shows. Also important is figuring out when you should come back. Give yourself a month to start with. Take another month off if you still do not feel ready to return, but then return. You are retreating for your own good. You are not running away.

When you say that you are leaving, do not make a big deal about it. If someone asks, say that you wanted to try something different or that you needed a break. If you trust the person, you can admit to him or her that you need some time away from your ex, but ask him or her not to repeat that information. If he or she is your friend, he or she will not.

Chapter 4

The Ex Games

U p until now, we have talked about making a clean break from your ex. However, unless something drastic happens, like one of you leaves for a different city, the odds are good that you will see your ex again. At best, you will know ahead of time that your ex will show up, and the event will be large enough that you do not have to worry about running into him or her. At worst, you are stuck sharing a desk in your least favorite class with your ex while you struggle to forget him or her.

What should you do when you see your ex again? How should you behave? What if your ex is actively dating again? Oddly, relationship advice glosses over this part, perhaps thinking that you will act the usual way toward someone you do not want to see — polite but guarded. The problem is that when you see your ex again, your mind puts itself into overdrive trying to figure out what topics are safe to discuss, what you can and cannot say if you want to avoid fighting with your ex, and what your ultimate goal is. If that were not enough, there is also that nagging question of how to respond if your ex decides to start pushing your buttons.

Even though dealing with your ex can feel like walking in a minefield while barefoot, it does not have to be so difficult. There are things you can do to make interacting easier.

Set Boundaries

The first thing you can do is take time with your ex and flesh out the rules of engagement for when you see each other. Make rules about what will be discussed and what will not be shared. If you have a class together, agree to only talk to each other about school matters. This technique will work better if your breakup was mutual or at least performed civilly. Even if you cannot talk to your ex without managing to get into a fight, you can still draw up boundaries for yourself.

Sample boundaries are:

- Only talk about the matter at hand with your ex.

- Do not say anything about how your ex acted when you were together.

- Try not to say anything that will upset your ex.

- Avoid talking about your current relationship, or lack thereof.

These boundaries apply, regardless of where you two meet. If you go to the same martial arts dojo, practice with people other than your ex, and talk with other people before and after lessons. Do not actively avoid your ex, though. If he or she greets you, greet him or her back. If your ex asks how you are, you can say you are doing well. After that, you can politely excuse yourself.

How to Win a Fight With Your Ex

At this point, you are conjuring up mental images of your ex going through his or her catalog of best insults and verbal jabs for your next meeting. Setting boundaries and being polite are necessary, but what happens when you are with your friends and your ex makes a quick remark that you still have no fashion sense or reveals that you went through a time when you wanted to be a goth or a cheerleader, or just brings up the times you made a fool out of yourself in public? You want to answer back, and you have choice words of your own all saved up, ones that you have practiced in the mirror 20 times, just so you could get the last word in.

Do not give in to that temptation. If you get insulted or belittled by your ex, do not take the bait. As satisfying as fighting back might initially feel, this is one situation where you can only win if you refuse to fight. Your ex might be ready to make all sorts of remarks toward you, but like bullies, if your ex sees they are not having any effect, he or she is going to get tired of trying to hurt you. If you do decide to sink down to your ex's level, you are either going to get trounced because there are things you thought were off-limits that your ex has no problem bringing up, or you will beat your ex at his or her own game and look terrible in front of any onlookers — perhaps mutual friends, who are going to think your ex was right to break up with you; or your ex's new date, who will feel that your ex was right to break up with the crazy person; or your new date, who might start to put himself or herself in the place of your ex and think that going out with you again is a bad idea.

So what do you do? Keep being civil. At least one of you has to. This does not mean you have to let every insult go unanswered, though. If your ex says you tried to poison him or her with your cooking, you can point out that several people like your food. If your ex says you have terrible fashion sense, say you are sorry he or she thinks that or that you like the way you dress. If your ex brings up an embarrassing phase in your life, you can reply that everyone has an event like that in their past. Do not harp on it, though. Saying that everyone has made mistakes and then listing your ex's mistakes while dating you is not being civil — it is fighting. Your goal is to not get involved in the conflict. If this seems too difficult, consider this: If your ex continues attacking you or escalates his or her attacks, he or she is only going to be hurting himself or herself in the eyes of your classmates and friends.

Also, be civil when talking about your ex with your friends, even if your ex is not around. If you feel you must discuss your feelings with a friend, the first step is to try to keep the people who are friends with both you and your ex out of the conflict. Forcing your friends to choose sides is unfair to them. Second, if all the friends in whom you can confide are also friends with your ex, then it is time to gauge how trustworthy they are. Pick a friend who you know will keep your conversations confidential, and ask if you can discuss things with him or her. Make sure that nothing you say will get back to your ex. Also, avoid asking your friend if your ex has been saying anything about you.

Other Unhealthy Behaviors

You know how to behave around your ex, and you know how to at least act civil. Maybe you can even be genuinely polite. However, when you have to be around your ex, you are still reopening an old emotional wound — and like any open wound, it can get infected. This does not mean talking about negative emotions that are part of the healing process, such as anger or sadness. These emotions are unhealthy feelings, to the point that even if you can still manage to be polite toward your ex when you see him or her, you will not be able to move on. These emotions can sabotage all your future relationships. In extreme cases, these emotions might prevent you from having another relationship again.

Envy

The first unhealthy feeling to overcome is envy. The best description of envy comes from the researchers W. Gerrod Parrott and Richard Smith, who write that envy is an emotion "that occurs when a person lacks another's (perceived) superior quality, achievement, or possession and desires it or wishes that the other lacked it." In relationships, it is the feeling you get when you see your ex doing better than you.

Despite what you might believe, envy is not jealousy. Whereas envy is wanting what someone else has, jealousy is a fear that someone might take away something you have, such as a boyfriend or girlfriend.

Although wanting what someone else has is not bad, the problem with envy is that it makes you unhappy, to the point where you want to inflict that pain on other people. Envy can also result in taking pleasure in your ex's misfortunes.

THE GREEN-EYED MONSTER

Why do we call jealousy and envy a "green-eyed monster?" Why does someone turn green with envy? You can thank William Shakespeare for that. The earliest time jealousy is referred to as green-eyed is in the 1596 play "The Merchant of Venice," where Portia talks about "green-eyed jealousy." In his 1603 play "Othello," the character Iago says, "O, beware, my lord, of jealousy, it is the green-eyed monster which doth mock the meat it feeds on." Because envy is similar to jealousy, it also became associated with the color green.

Other people might have used this term before Shakespeare, but he is the one who first wrote it. So if you come up with a clever metaphor and a friend uses it in a play, make sure he or she gives you proper credit.

Why should envy and jealousy be green, though? This is likely because the color green is associated with sickness and rot. For instance, another old saying is that someone who is sick looks a little green around the gills. Also, moldy food looks green, too. Even back in Shakespeare's time, jealousy was considered unhealthy.

Overcoming Envy

On the surface, overcoming envy seems impossible. How do you make yourself not want something? If you convince yourself you do not want something you know you wanted, aren't you deluding yourself?

The truth is that when you work to overcome envy, you are not deluding yourself. Instead, you look at the reality of the situation differently and put a more positive spin on them. One of the best ways to do this is to use your feelings of envy as a motivator to achieve your goals. For instance, if your ex has a new cellphone the next time you see him or her, you can use the envy you feel to spur you to start looking for a cellphone of your own. If you see your ex with a boyfriend or girlfriend who looks as though he or she is a supermodel, use those feelings to drive you to get a supermodel-looking boyfriend or girlfriend of your own.

However, before you go rushing off to get whatever your ex has, ask yourself why you feel envious. Do you want a new cellphone, or do you want to show off how well you are doing to your ex? Although having a new boyfriend or girlfriend who looks like a supermodel is nice to think about, maybe you are more bothered that your ex seems to have traded you for a nicer model — no pun intended. When you know the cause of your envy, you will have a clearer idea of the goal you want to achieve. Maybe getting a new cellphone is something you could do without. Maybe getting a part-time job and earning enough that you could get a new cellphone if you wanted is a better goal. As far as the supermodel, you can shoot for the stars there. You might want to consider, though, that your real goal is to find someone who makes you happy, which is the reason you become envious when you see your ex dating a supermodel.

Another way to overcome envy is to consider the positive side to not having what your ex has. So your ex has a new cellphone? Just consider all the money that must be leaving his or her hands after buying the cellphone and paying for a data plan — money that is staying in your pocket instead of being eaten up by a new cellphone plan. If your ex is dating a guy or girl who looks like a supermodel, remember that he or she is eating up all his or her free time. You, on the other hand, have time to hit the gym or play that new video game, or get through *Pride and Prejudice*. In other words, you can focus on you because in relationships, personal time can be scarce.

Aside from thinking of the positive side to not having what your ex has, think about the positives you have. You might be extremely smart, for instance. You might also have an adventurous streak people lack, or you could be a skilled singer. Perhaps you are extremely coordinated, you have a good part-time job, or you play the violin very well. There are aspects of you that would make other people envious, too.

The final thing to consider when overcoming envy is that everyone has their positives and their negatives. Think about this — someone might be envious of you. Maybe right now someone is wishing he or she had your taste in clothes, your sense of humor, or even your hair or eyes. Are you wondering why someone would ever be envious of something you possess? Chances are the person you are envying feels the same way. He or she can see the big picture about himself or herself, positive and negative, and he or she is envious of someone who has what he or she lacks. If your ex is trying to make you feel envious, think about how insecure he or she must be that he or she has to try to make people feel envious. If your ex's sense of self-worth is so wrapped up in what other people think, it does not say much about his or her self-confidence or self-esteem.

When you think about envy, you realize that everyone has something enviable about them, and that everyone can be envious about something they lack in their lives. What matters is how you feel about yourself.

Bitterness

If there is one sentiment to avoid more than envy, it is bitterness — also known as resentment. You will find different definitions of what bitterness is, but in relationships, bitterness is envy mixed with anger — despising other people for what they have that you lack. Resentment and bitterness result from something you feel is unfair, such as feeling as though your accomplishments are not being recognized, or that others are taking advantage of you. Humiliation also sparks bitterness, especially if you are publicly humiliated or if you are forced to take the humiliation without saying anything.

Just thinking about your breakup can lead to resentment, let alone actually meeting up with your ex. Although becoming resentful is easy when your ex insults you and belittles you while you are trying to be civil, you can just as easily become bitter and resentful listening to your ex tell your friends about how his or her life has been since he or she broke up with you.

One of the problems with resenting someone is that it is easy to do. All you have to do is dwell on the events that have left you hurt and angry, and when your heart has been broken, that is entirely what you feel like doing.

Another problem with bitterness is that it will hurt you more than anyone else. The longer you stay resentful, the more you put up an emotional barrier that stops you from forming good relationships between you and any prospective new friends or romantic interests. What is worse, bitterness can also consume you to the point where you stop growing. It can shred your self-confidence and sabotage your attempts to trust other people and make you become reluctant to reveal information about yourself to people. It leaves you so focused on the hurt you suffered that you become unable to enjoy the present.

Effects that are even more long-term include realizing that you are lacking a purpose in life, and that your view of the world has somehow been altered so that it conflicts with what is commonly accepted to be true. For instance, if you believe in the inherent goodness of humanity, you might be surprised to discover that you live your life expecting other people will attack you if you are so stupid as to reveal too much of yourself to them.

HOW CAN YOU TELL IF YOU ARE RESENTFUL?

How can you tell if you are feeling bitter over your breakup? After all, feeling angry and sad are natural parts of the grieving process. At what point do those feelings turn into resentment? Here is a quick guide:

- Do you have to fake being happy while you are around your ex when you would rather scream at him or her?

- Do you have to watch yourself to make sure you do not insult your ex or become sarcastic?

- Do you have nightmares about your ex?

- Do you get angry, seemingly without a reason?

- Do you become edgy when you start thinking about your ex?

- Do you get upset when something reminds you of your ex, such as a song, a restaurant you went to, or a certain movie?

If you find yourself nodding in recognition, you might have a problem with bitterness.

Overcoming Bitterness

Becoming bitter is easy. Getting over bitterness is less so. The first thing you have to do is want to change. If you are feeling resentful toward your ex, ask yourself if you feel good about that. Is it giving you any satisfaction, or is it stripping the happiness out of your day? At this point, be aware that it is hurting you. So think back to the last time you felt happy, before you started resenting your ex. Wouldn't it be nice to feel that good again? Wouldn't it be nice to get on with your life and have your ex be surprised at how well you are doing, instead of the other way around? You can get there, but you have to make the choice to reject being bitter or jealous.

CASE STUDY: TIPS FROM AN OPRAH EXPERT

Sharon Rivkin, M.A., M.F.T., has been featured in notable publications, such as O: The Oprah Magazine, Reader's Digest, and Yahoo.com. She has also appeared on "Martha Stewart Whole Living Radio." Here are her tips on getting through a breakup, "whether you left or were left."

TO GET THROUGH A BREAKUP:

1. Create a good support system that includes friends and family. Think about who will be understanding, nonjudgmental, and willingly supportive, then give them a call. If there is someone who has been through something similar, put him or her at the top of your call list.

2. Seek out professional help if you can. This is a necessity if you are extremely depressed and/or anxious or terribly guilt-ridden (if you were the one who left the relationship). The more you know about yourself and your core issues, the better you will heal, learn something from the relationship, and not make the same mistakes in the next one. This is a learning experience, not a conspiracy to make you miserable.

3. Find out your core issue by using the three-step, First Argument Technique system. It reveals critical information about yourself that will help you understand the "why," the "what," and the "how" about you and your relationships. Why do I keep choosing the wrong partner? What is my past telling me that will help me with future relationships? How can I use this information to make positive changes in myself and my relationships?

4. Absorb yourself in good self-help books, and be grateful about what you have, rather than just focusing on what you do not have or have lost.

5. Remember that you are grieving and it takes time to feel good again — even if you are the one that ended the relationship. It is hard either way.

6. If you were left, remember all the things you were not happy with. It is not all one-sided. This will help you not to feel like a victim.

7. Take care of yourself — treat yourself to a massage or facial, exercise, or do whatever makes you feel better.

Take this day-by-day. Stay in the present, and do not worry about tomorrow. Your feelings and emotions about the breakup are going to be all over the place. You need all the support, information and tools you can get at this difficult time. But know that there is a beginning, middle and an end to this.

DO NOT:

1. Do not try to get information about your ex. You might think you want to know his or her every move, but it will only make things worse.

2. Do not have contact with your ex — less is better in this situation. If you left, do not alleviate your guilt by "checking in". If you have been left, time and space will help you heal and feel yourself again.

3. Do not spend time with people who you feel are judgmental or too opinionated. You want support and honesty with compassion at this time, not necessarily advice.

4. Do not put the relationship or your ex on a pedestal. Remember the truth about the relationship and what was not working. If you left, this will help with your guilt. If you were left, this will help you feel less like a victim.

HOW TO COPE AFTER SEEING YOUR EX:

1. Know that it will stir up your feelings — good or bad — again, and it will take time to get back to coping and getting through the breakup.

2. Call your support system to talk.

3. Once again, remember the truth about the relationship and the reasons why you have broken up.

4. Get back into present time as soon as possible. It is hard to see your ex again, but it is over.

5. Cry, scream, whatever; express your feelings. Once you love someone, you do not automatically forget him or her or your feelings. Breaking up is hard to do, so cut yourself slack if you find yourself moving backward after seeing your ex.

Forget Waiting — Forgiveness is the Hardest Part

Deciding you need to move on is one thing. Doing it is another because to do so you have to forgive your ex for all the pain he or she inflicted on you, something that ranks below sticking a hand in a shark tank for many people.

What seems so insulting about having to forgive an ex you are resentful of is that you know he or she was wrong. Whether your ex did inconsiderate things, such as copying your homework assignments instead of working on them together or betrayed you by dating someone else while you were together, the fact remains — if you forgive him or her, that means he or she gets away with hurting you.

First, forgiving your ex is not about doing something nice for him or her, it is about doing something nice for you. If that seems wrong, ask yourself how your ex is suffering because you resent him or her? The answer is that unless your ex cares what you think of him or her, he or she is not suffering. This gives you three options: You can spend your time resenting your ex and hoping something bad will happen to him or her; you could take matters into your own hands and make something bad happen to your ex; or you can choose to let him or her move on. The first option guarantees that you will be thinking of your ex for a long time, and the second will haunt you for the rest of your life. The third option is the only way for you to get over him or her.

So how do you forgive? On paper, it is pretty easy. You choose to forgive your ex and move on. In practice, it is harder. Forgiving someone means when you think about them and feel envious or resentful, you choose to let go and concentrate on other things, such as doing something good for yourself. It is not easy, and contrary to every romance movie in existence, there is not one moment when you forgive someone and move on. Instead, one day you wake up and realize as a passing thought that you do not resent your ex anymore, and that thought brightens your day as you head out into the world to live your life.

THERE IS NO TIME FOR REVENGE

One of the favorite concepts in fiction is someone getting revenge for a wrong. Hamlet gets his revenge on Claudius for killing his father, for example. Arnold Schwarzenegger's villains have all done something that merited revenge, and several romantic comedies have a villain who gets his or her just punishment at the end of the movie.

Real-life revenge, though, has to deal with an aftermath that fiction ignores. While the fantasy is that things go back to normal once you have exacted your revenge, the truth is that when you get revenge on someone, you might have to do things you did not think you would do. Therapist Michael Etts notes that revenge entails acts that, at best, require you to be indifferent to human suffering. At worst, it requires cruelty and the ability to enjoy someone else's suffering. Dealing with these acts can be more traumatic than the events that drove you to seek revenge, and researcher Judith Herman's 1992 research noted that revenge can case post-traumatic stress disorder (PTSD). There is also the problem of your ex wanting to get revenge on you after you have gotten your revenge on him or her. If your revenge is severe enough, you might also have to explain your actions to a judge.

Take, for example, revenge porn. During your relationship, you and your ex may have sent one another sexually explicit photos, or sexted. Although it may seem like a good way to get back at your ex at the time, posting these pictures online to social media accounts or pornography websites can be damaging to the both of you. Aside from the severe emotional trauma such a breach of privacy would cause your ex, posting such pictures could land you in jail on child pornography charges if your ex is under the age of 18. Revenge porn is never the answer.

Even though forgiveness can be difficult, there are tips that can make the decision easier, or at least less hard.

You are not condoning your ex's behavior. The important thing to remember about forgiveness is that you are not letting your ex get away with his or her behavior. When you think about forgiving your ex, make sure the term does not mean, "letting him or her get away with hurting me." Instead, make sure the term means, "not letting him or her continue to hurt me." That is your ultimate goal, and it feels better to think of forgiveness that way. Forgiving your ex is about helping you to let go and move on.

Think about the best way to achieve revenge on your ex. This might seem a little contradictory, but consider this: Is the best revenge against your ex sitting around and thinking about how much you despise his or her job, significant other, and all the things he or she has that you lack? Or would a better revenge be running into your ex years later with a boyfriend or girlfriend, a job, and tastefully showing off your acquired fame or wealth? If you need another incentive, consider the fact that only one of those choices will affect your ex.

Another good way to get revenge is by making your breakup the best thing that happened to you. If you feel that your ex was trying to hurt you or was being insensitive when he or she broke up with you, ask yourself what will give your ex more power. Is it the view that he or she was such an amazing boyfriend or girlfriend that him or her breaking up with you wrecked your life forever? Or is it the view that your ex did you more of a favor by leaving than he or she ever could have by staying with you? Once again, the choice is yours.

Stop dwelling on the pain. Think about the past two weeks. Have your thoughts been on your ex? Have you talked with someone about how much you dislike your ex or all the ways in which he or she hurt you? The more you come back and relive the pain you have felt, the more you will resent your ex and the harder forgiving will be. To help combat this, look at the situation from your ex's perspective. Stand in front of a mirror and start to tell the story as your ex might have experienced it. This is not an easy thing to do, but when you try to see things from a different point of view, you are shifting your perspective and allowing yourself to empathize, even if the subject is not someone you particularly care to empathize with.

Realize that your ex is a person, too. While you might despise your ex, remember he or she is more than just your former boyfriend or girlfriend. Just realizing that might soften up the image you have of him or her in your head. This exercise is to be used to see your ex in a different light, not to make you miss him or her again.

Look for positive signs. The more focused you are on negativity, the harder forgiving your ex will be. To counteract this, think about the positive outcomes. Granted, this can be hard when you have been stuck in a negative mindset for so long, so start small. Come up with just one positive thing that has happened as a result of your breakup. It does not have to be something big. It might just be the fact that you got to do something you liked that your ex did not, such as going to see a chick flick or trying a new Mexican restaurant with friends or family.

If you can come up with one positive, try more. Try to list 10 good things that have happened to you as a result of the breakup. If you are having trouble, here are examples:

- Something you bought after the breakup that you had wanted for a while

- A new hobby you began

- A goal you have achieved, such as regularly going to the gym

- How much your family and friends have stepped up to care for you

- A visit you took to your favorite restaurant with your family or friends

- A new opportunity of which you took advantage

- A new project you began

- New friends that you made

- New groups you joined

- Bad habits you quit

Wish for good things to happen to your ex. Even though this might be the last thing in the world you feel like doing, try it. When you start to think about your ex and how he or she wronged you, wish him or her well. Make a habit of doing this, and you will hope that something good happens to them without feeling as though you mean the exact opposite. This trick works in part because it forces you to look at your ex in a different light, as someone who might be deserving of well wishes and not someone to be resented.

Give yourself permission to make mistakes. You already know that forgiveness is an ongoing process. You should also be aware that, like any ongoing project, there will be times when you fail to meet your expectations. You might look at the positives and dismiss them outright. Or you might wish your ex well by hoping he or she gets hit by a car, since that will teach him or her the value of looking both ways before crossing the street. Even though these are things you would not tell anyone else, after you have thought them, you might feel discouraged. Instead, be understanding. Remember that you are not perfect, that you have been angry with your ex, and that these feelings take time to get over. If you give in to feeling resentful or envious, acknowledge that you fell off the forgiveness wagon, and then make sure you keep trying. If you beat yourself up, you will be less likely to continue trying to forgive your ex. This will keep you feeling resentful. Take it easy on yourself. Try again, and remember that the important thing is to keep trying until you succeed.

A LITTLE HELP, PLEASE?

If you are not making any headway in forgiving your ex and your friends and family are not helping, you might want to consider talking with a religious leader. Forgiveness is an essential part of religions, and religious leaders in the community — such as pastors, priests, rabbis, or imams — are used to being counselors. If you do not feel comfortable talking to a religious leader, talk your issues over with a therapist or psychologist.

Stalking

No jokes or cleverness here — stalking is bad. According to Yale University, stalking is defined as "a pattern of repeated and unwanted attention, harassment, contact, or any other course of conduct directed at a specific person that would cause a reasonable person to feel fear." It is illegal in the United States. What leads to the temptation is understandable. You want your ex to know that even if he or she broke your heart, your ex cannot just pretend that your relationship did not exist. And what better way is there to do that than by constantly reminding him or her that you exist? It is a small step from reminding him or her you exist to stalking, and if you cross that line, you need to stop. Here are steps to help you.

1. The first step is to admit you are stalking someone. While you might feel that doing something as simple as going out of your way to drive by his or her house or changing your habits to shop in the same stores as your ex are not big deals, the fact is that most people would not do this. It is one thing to feel empty without your ex and pine over losing the relationship, but when you reach the stage that you repeatedly try to see or talk to him or her, you begin to cross the line into stalker territory.

2. Figure out what to do with the time you spent stalking your ex. Like any bad habit, once a stalker decides to stop, he or she will need to let something else occupy his or her thoughts. Doing volunteer work can help, and it is also a good way for someone who has been stalking someone else to feel as though he or she is doing something to help other people. In other words, it is a good way to start feeling redeemed.

3. See a psychologist if this behavior becomes compulsive. Stalking might be a symptom of depression or a host of personality disorders, such as avoidant personality disorder, dependency, borderline personality disorder or even antisocial personality disorder. It might also be a symptom of a full-blown psychotic mental illness. The bottom line is that if you cannot make yourself quit stalking, then the best thing for you to do is talk with a professional.

4. When you have managed to quit stalking your ex, you need to forgive yourself. You might look back on your period of stalking your ex and wonder just what you were thinking, but do not let what you did in the past influence who you are in the present. Besides, you managed to overcome that part of yourself. You have conquered this behavior, and that says something about you.

And now, a view from the other side...

Up to now, you have been reading about how to behave around your ex and how to curb your own worst impulses. Now, however, the focus shifts to your ex. What do you do if your ex starts making threats against you? What if he or she starts stalking you? What if your ex hits you in retaliation for breaking up?

Putting a Stop to Blackmail

You might not like dealing with snide comments and insults your ex makes, but you can brush them off and show your ex you refuse to let him or her hurt you. What happens, though, if your ex decides to blackmail you or threaten you?

Being blackmailed, while uncomfortable, can be solved relatively easily. If your ex attempts to blackmail you, first let him or her know blackmail is illegal. Then let your ex know that you would rather tell people yourself about the blackmail material than have him or her show it. Relationship blackmail material might be embarrassing or explicit pictures, so tell people about the blackmail materials before your ex can show them. Unfortunately, this will be embarrassing, but by doing this you take away the power they have over you and leave your ex with nothing. Just saying you will tell people about the blackmail material should be enough to stop your ex from using it.

Threats and Abuse

When your ex decides to stop insulting you and start threatening you, bring in other people. Contact your family, alert them to the situation, and ask them to walk with you when you do errands or go out. If you believe your ex is capable of following through on his or her threats, you might want to get the police involved. According to attorney Stacy D. Phillips, though, you need to gather evidence against your ex. Save the threatening voice mails or notes he or she sends you. However, some state laws prevent you from recording conversations unless you have your ex's permission.

The police should also be involved if your ex hits you. That is not just abuse; it is assault. Tell your family, go to the police and file a criminal report. At the very least, get a restraining order. You have heard stories or seen movies about vengeful exes and stalkers walking through a restraining order when they find out one has been placed on them, but the reality, according to Stacy Phillips, is that once people find out the law has gotten involved, they will finally be shocked back into the real world.

 **SELF-DEFENSE**

If you're concerned about the threats of an ex, it may be a good idea to enroll yourself in a self-defense class. Although you should definitely tell your family and alert the police first if you are worried, taking self-defense lessons may help to make you feel safer.

Many police departments offer self-defense classes, especially those located in college towns. If your local police department does not teach self-defense, look into your local martial arts studios for special self-defense classes. While the need to learn to defend yourself may be frightening, self-defense classes can be empowering. Go with friends and family to make the experience less intimidating.

If you don't like the idea of attending a live self-defense class, consider searching the Web for videos and articles about defense tips. Although a live class may be the best option, these can still be helpful .

Self-defense classes aren't just for women. Although there are a number of women-specific classes, there are defense classes offered for both sexes. Don't let your gender stop you from learning tactics to defend yourself if you feel it is necessary.

When You are Being Stalked

All the advice about what to do if your ex threatens you or hits you applies equally to an ex that begins stalking you. There are more things you can do to discourage stalking, though. First, confront the stalker when he or she shows up. Tell your ex in no uncertain terms that you want him or her to leave you alone. After that, treat your ex like any other bully trying to get under your skin and refuse to talk to him or her when he or she shows up somewhere unannounced. Stalkers take any interaction as approval for what they are doing, so do not give him or her that approval. Walk past your ex if he or she shows up in your neighborhood or in your local grocery store. Return any mail or packages your ex sends you, hang up if he or she calls, and send all of his or her emails to your junk mail folder.

You will also want to tell everyone you know, especially your family, that your ex is stalking you. Stalkers work best when they think they are being secretive. Letting everyone know that your ex is stalking you will take away that advantage. Also, the fact that other people know what your ex is doing might be enough to shame him or her into quitting.

If that is not enough, you might have to acknowledge that your ex might pose a threat to you. Take extra precautions. You might need to change your phone number and your daily routines. Then start collecting information and let the police know.

THE FIVE KINDS OF STALKERS

In 1999, a team of researchers led by Paul Mullen studied the different types of stalkers. From their research, they identified five categories into which stalkers fall:

- A **predatory stalker** stalks his or her victim to attack (meaning "rape") them.

- An **intimacy seeker** believes that he or she and the victim were meant to be together. He or she tries to create a loving relationship between him- or herself and the victim.

- An **incompetent suitor** is a stalker who is fixated on developing a relationship, despite the fact that his or her victim is dating someone else.

- A **rejected stalker** is trying to rectify or avenge a divorce, a breakup, or perhaps even being fired.

- A **resentful stalker** wants to terrify and inflict mental pain on his or her victim, against whom he or she is holding a grudge.

Later research done by the National Victim Assistance Academy has come up with a sixth kind of stalker. The **vengeance/terrorist stalker** is different than other stalkers because he or she is looking to force the victim to do something, whether it is get involved with an extremist group or to punish the victim for a perceived wrong committed against the stalker.

Seeing your ex again can feel like navigating a minefield. Unlike minefields, though, you can manage to navigate through this without getting hurt. Better yet, when you are not worried about what will happen between you and your ex the next time you see her, you are free to spend all that mental effort on something truly worthwhile — improving yourself.

Chapter 5

How to Not Let Yourself Go Mentally

One of the annoying aspects of getting your heart broken is how all-encompassing it can become. Thinking about your breakup and mentally replaying your relationship in your head to try to sort it out is natural. So is considering the ways in which you could change to win your ex back. As long as you are focused on that, however, you are not moving on. You need to take care of yourself, mentally and physically.

Your mental state is important. A negative mental state will make getting over your heartbreak harder. A negative attitude can make it impossible. On the other hand, if you can maintain a positive state, getting over your breakup will be easier. As an added bonus, it can give you stability and psychological strength that will serve you well and make getting through future problems easier. The best part is that there are ways to keep yourself mentally fit.

Self Esteem: A Primer

First thing's first — one of the casualties during a breakup is your self-esteem. There are ways that it manifests, from taking all the blame for the breakup because "I wasn't a good boyfriend" to staring at yourself in the mirror and picking out all your physical flaws. Then, there is the self-doubt that, if your ex, who knew you as intimately as your family did, rejected you, then maybe you do not have anything to offer in a relationship. Asking yourself these questions and treating yourself like something you might find in a dumpster can create mental wounds that take a long time to heal.

This problem is not helped by the fact that low self-esteem is common in Americans in general. It is even encouraged. Americans qualify the compliments people give them, downplay their accomplishments and beat themselves up over their mistakes more than they praise themselves for their triumphs. Fortunately, there are resources available to help you patch up your self-esteem and make you feel good about who you are. Below are effective tips to help you bandage up those emotional wounds and feel better about yourself:

1. **List your strengths.** Everyone has them, including you. If you are not sure what your strengths are, ask people who know you, such as your friends or family. Your family in particular is the best resource for discovering your strengths. Find at least four or five strengths, write them

down and put the list in a safe place where you can look at it, such as a desk drawer. You might also want to make a travel copy to keep in your backpack or wallet. Remind yourself of them. For instance, if you are feeling down because you cannot play basketball well, remind yourself that you have a sense of humor. If you feel depressed because you do not think you are a good writer, remind yourself that you are good at playing the trumpet.

2. **Remember that nobody is perfect.** This can be the hardest thing to do, especially if you are comparing yourself to someone who is more popular than you. Although you might be able to see all the ways in which you fall short, remember that other person has flaws too. Maybe you have not heard her sing because she cannot carry a tune with two hands and a net. Maybe he is bad at math or is scared of dogs. You have your strengths and he or she has his or hers.

3. **Concentrate on improving your strengths.** Think about what you can do to improve your strengths. Maybe you could write a short story or create your own stand-up comedy routine. Find a project that corresponds with your strengths and work on it. The project does not have to be big. Getting an A on the next math test is acceptable. So is making dinner for your parents or cleaning your desk.

4. **Celebrate your victories.** When you succeed at something, take a moment to congratulate yourself. People succeed at a project and refuse to let themselves feel good, even for a little while because they are afraid

other people might see them as being arrogant. Forget that attitude. When you finish a project or succeed at a task, congratulate yourself. If you get an A on that math test, take time and feel good about what you did. If you baked cookies that turned out well, celebrate your master baking skills. You deserve to feel good after succeeding.

5. **Stretch your limits and impress yourself.** Do something you did not think you could do. Take a dance class, read something at a poetry slam, or even volunteer at a homeless shelter. Nothing raises self-esteem like doing something you did not think you could do. You will impress yourself, and while you are busy being impressed, celebrate the fact that you succeeded in going beyond your limits.

6. **Stay away from negativity.** People will be more than happy to take you down if they think you are not doing a good enough job on your own. It is easy to criticize someone else, and a sad truth is that people will rush to put you down just to make themselves feel better. During a speech in Paris in 1910, President Teddy Roosevelt had something to say about this:

   "It is not the critic who counts: not the man who points out how the strong man stumbles or where the doer of deeds could have done better. The credit belongs to the man who is in the arena, whose face is marred by dust and sweat and blood."

   It is easier to criticize. Do not hang around these people if you can help it. Instead, make an effort to be with people who appreciate you. Your family is the best source of positive emotions and praise.

7. **Stop thinking negative thoughts.** Once you have stopped other people from unduly criticizing you, take the next step and stop thinking negative thoughts about yourself. If you keep thinking you cannot succeed or will not be a good boyfriend or girlfriend, you will not. Your negative thoughts will lead to failure, a phenomenon known as a self-fulfilling prophecy. When you catch yourself thinking negative thoughts, stop yourself. Take a one-minute break and calm yourself down. You might want to try breathing deeply to help. Then acknowledge that you have limitations, but also say something positive about yourself. For instance, if you are thinking that you will be a bad boyfriend or girlfriend because you get tongue-tied, admit that you do not always know the right thing to say. But then tell yourself that despite being tongue-tied, you can remember important dates, such as birthdays and anniversaries.

8. **Honestly assess your weaknesses.** When you feel you have stopped the negativity in your life, you can look at yourself and honestly assess your weaknesses. However, do not let yourself be discouraged by them. Instead, accept that they exist, and if they trouble you, start brainstorming ways in which you can overcome these weaknesses. If you are bad at staying on top of your homework, make a commitment to yourself that you will record all of your assignments in a planner and assign a date by which you will complete them. Above all, you

are working on improving your weaknesses because it makes you feel good, not because you are worthless until you overcome your weaknesses.

9. **Learn to appreciate yourself.** No matter who you are, you do something every day that you can be proud of. Learn to spot those things and feel good about yourself for doing them. Maybe you are well organized. Maybe you finally understood that troublesome physics problem. Maybe you just made your bed before leaving in the morning. No matter what it is, take time during the day and celebrate those little accomplishments.

10. **Do not expect an overnight change.** Raising your self-esteem is a process. It will take time to establish the habits of congratulating yourself and focusing on your strengths rather than your weaknesses. Do not be discouraged, though. Instead of focusing on the big picture of your self-esteem, just concentrate on the little day-to-day goals. By the time you make those goals a habit, you will be surprised at how much better you feel about yourself, and you will feel better about walking up to people and starting conversations with them.

Take a Break

As you start to get your mental state into shape, give yourself a rest. Depending on where you are in the grieving process after the breakup, you might be feeling as though you want to crawl under the covers for the rest of the day, or you might want to move on from this grieving process at the mental equivalent of a sprint. Avoid these extremes. After all, when you have a broken leg, you do not start running as soon as the cast comes off. Similarly, you do not want to overexert a bruised ego.

First, take a break from the grieving process. At the beginning of the breakup, give yourself the time you need to feel terrible. After one or two weeks, though, give the grieving process a rest. Do something nice for yourself instead. It does not have to be something big or expensive, either. During the weekday, you can go to meet a friend or relative at a nice restaurant for dinner, swing by a bookstore, or just take a quick run to the ice cream store. Outside work or classes, do something more substantial, like taking a quick jog, getting a manicure or a massage, or just going window-shopping at the mall.

Later, when you start applying the techniques in this chapter, take time out from working to improve yourself. Do something mindless, such as watching episodes of your favorite TV series or a movie. Take time out and read that book you bought. For that matter, give yourself an hour or two to just surf the Internet.

Dear Diary...

Keeping a journal can have a positive effect on your mental health, and it can help you come to terms with your thoughts and feelings and help you understand what you are feeling in the first place. When you write down your thoughts, you are giving them order instead of having them swirling in your mind. You can write down how you are angry and why, or why you feel depressed. The best part is that once you have those thoughts down, you can look over them and start making plans on how to counter them.

Your journal can also help you keep track of how you progress through your breakup. If you find yourself writing down the same problem, you can devote more time to solving it and have an idea of what works and what does not. When you start to get over your breakup, you can then use your journal to write about your goals and make yourself a road map for your future.

You will need...

A pen and paper. That is it. Having the paper bound will help, so get a notebook or something similar. Because this is your journal and you want to make a habit of writing in it every day, you will want to make sure that the pen and notebook are ones that appeal to you. Some people like to have a three-subject notebook, while others go for a leather-bound journal. Some people like to carry around a fancy pen, while others get by with a standard No. 2 pencil. So go shopping at an office supply store, a supermarket, or a bookstore and see what notebooks appeal to you. Then select a pen you like, and get writing.

What to write about

One of the joys of journaling is that you can write about anything. If you are having trouble getting started, you can use a technique called free writing. Creative writers use it to get themselves started, and it is a valuable tool for keeping a journal.

To free write, all you have to do is have a writing prompt, a question or thought you can write about. Because you are getting over a breakup, "How do you feel?" could be a good prompt. "How was your day today?" could also work. These prompts can keep a person journaling forever. Once you start writing, do not try to compose your thoughts into perfect sentences. Any and all grammatical mistakes are permissible. So are misspellings. Do not interrupt the flow of your words to look up a word in the dictionary. The important thing is to keep up the flow of your words until you feel you are finished. After you have become more comfortable with keeping a journal, you can take a more structured approach to your journal entries if you wish. Even when you feel there is nothing to talk about, you can find something to say about how you are feeling.

Affirm the Positive

According to grief counselor Susan Elliott, one of the tools for helping to restore your self-esteem is using affirmations — constant repetition of positive statements. Like other techniques to keep your mental spirits up, affirmation seems simple, but it will only work if you keep doing it. Affirmations, if used correctly, can be a powerful way to restore your self-esteem and give you more self-esteem than you have ever had before.

How does it work?

Affirmations affect your subconscious, the area of your mind that develops your self-image, along with your skills, habits and other personality quirks. These aspects of your mind have one thing in common — they are made stronger by repetition. That is because your subconscious mind is simple and habitual. It takes statements at face value and does not understand anything presented to it negatively. It also only understands simple concepts, and even then those concepts have to be presented to it one at a time.

The subconscious mind takes in and imprints things that are presented to it, so repeating messages will cause it to embrace those messages, good or bad. For instance, if a teacher in elementary school says you are intelligent and keeps repeating it, over time, being intelligent will be a part of your self-image. The same thing goes for negative messages, such as your ex calling you immature. Over time, you might come to believe you are immature and struggle to be more mature. Unfortunately, erasing an imprint from your subconscious is not easy. However, when you realize how your subconscious works, you can figure out how to "program" your subconscious. In doing so, you can change how you think about yourself.

RISKY BUSINESS?

One of the common fears regarding affirmations and other practices that are supposed to alter your subconscious is the idea that if you try to alter the way you think, something will go horribly wrong and you will not be you anymore. Fortunately, this fear has no basis. Affirmations are not strong enough to do that. A fear that something like this will happen is the result of a fear of change. If you have lived with the conception that you are not self-confident, for instance, the idea of you as a self-confident person is alien to you. You start to think of people who you know are self-confident and stereotypes of what a self-confident person acts like, and you begin to wonder if your personality can survive a change like this or if you even want to become this new person.

Rest assured, your personality is not going to go anywhere. If anything, changing your subconscious' image of yourself will make your personality more powerful, not less.

If that does not convince you, think of a personality trait you would like to change. Maybe you want to be more responsible, less afraid of asking people out, or less shy in groups.

Now imagine yourself as a more responsible person. Imagine yourself confidently talking to a group and having everyone's attention. Imagine that you can go up to your dream date and strike up a conversation, mentioning that you would love to talk with him or her more over dinner. After you have finished imagining, ask yourself if you were a massively different person in the scenario you dreamed up or if you were just yourself, but a more ideal version of you.

To be fair, there are practices you should be wary of testing on yourself. For instance, while self-hypnosis is popular, you might want to discuss using it with a psychologist or physician who is familiar with the practice. You will not accidentally erase your personality while hypnotizing yourself, but you should get professional advice about what you are getting into.

The real problem with talking to yourself

People talk to themselves constantly, almost from the moment they get up until the moment they go to sleep. We talk to ourselves about decisions we will make throughout the day, what things we will talk about with other people, and when we are finished, we examine how we acted and assess our performance. This self-examination and self-assessment is unfavorable, bordering on cruel. We call ourselves names when we are running late, if we say something awkward, if we make a mistake on an exam, or if a work project is not perfect. "I can't believe I was late for work today," you might say. "I am such an idiot." The problem is that telling yourself this sends your subconscious the message that you are stupid, which then becomes part of your self-image.

Talking negatively about yourself is a common habit, but it is one that needs to be stopped. After all, people make mistakes. They forget to do something or arrive late or say something they should not or promise to do something they realize they cannot do. When you make a mistake, though, you internalize it and let that mistake erode your self-image. Ultimately, that leads to you feeling worthless and settling for less than you wanted, including romantic partners who are less than ideal.

To improve your self-esteem, you have to stop with these vicious self-assessments and the constant stream of negativity. The problem, though, is that you are still going to talk to yourself. This is where affirmations come in.

What affirmations are and how to use them

Affirmations are quick bursts of positive reinforcement, sentences you can use to combat the negative messages you send to yourself with positive ones. For instance, "I am intelligent," and "I have a strong work ethic," are examples of affirmations. These affirmations fall into three categories.

The **self-soothing affirmation** strengthens the positive aspects of your self-image. This helps you feel better about yourself by drawing away attention from the negative aspects. Examples of self-soothing affirmations are statements such as, "I have a nice smile," or "I am good with computers."

Self-soothing affirmations are ways to overcome feelings of depression, anger, or anxiety, and they can also be used to counter the effects of a bad day, or to make you feel better about the work you are doing to meet your goals. You can tell yourself, "I can make it through today," or "I am handling the difficulties of the day effectively," to make it through a bad day. Statements such as, "I am getting over this breakup," and "I am discovering new, positive things about myself," are affirmations that remind you the work you are doing is paying off.

Where self-soothing affirmations reinforce good feelings about yourself, **image-improvement affirmations** are designed to focus your mind on changes you want to see in yourself and can be used to change part of your self-image or one specific area.

Examples of image-improvement affirmations include:

- I am assertive.
- I have clean teeth.
- I have nice hair.
- I have impeccable taste in jackets.

Finally, **action affirmations** are designed to get you into the frame of mind of doing a certain action as part of a series of steps to reach your goals. You can tell yourself, "I practice juggling for a half-hour a day," if you want to be an expert juggler, or "I make 15 history flashcards every day," if you want to prepare yourself to ace an upcoming exam.

Preparation: What did you just say to me?

The first step is to take the journal you have been writing in and make a new section. Then spend one day and listen to what you say to yourself. Capture the positive self-talk and the negative. You want as clear a picture as you can possibly get about what you say to yourself. What do you say to yourself as you get in the shower to start another day? What do you say when you see yourself in the bathroom mirror? What are you telling yourself as you go to school, and what do you say throughout the school day and when you get home in the afternoon? Try to keep monitoring your observations until you go to bed, although you do not have to. The next day, look at what you tell yourself. Then, go through each negative statement and write in a positive substitute, something that addresses the same issue as the negative statement. If one of your negative comments is "I am ugly," you will need to replace it with an affirmation that says, "I look good."

The six characteristics of highly effective affirmations

When you write up your affirmations, word them so your subconscious mind will easily accept them. Think of it as though you are telling something to a small child that you want him or her to remember. Your affirmations have to be positive, personal, brief, corrective, present and concise.

Being positive is vital to your affirmation sticking. Your subconscious does not understand the concept of absence, so your affirmation has to refer to something positive. This might be the reason you did not listen when your mom would say that you were not a loser or were not ugly or whatever thing your classmates in elementary school might have said about you. Eliminate words such as "no" and "not" from your vocabulary when coming up with your affirmations. If your affirmation is something such as, "I am not fat," your subconscious will remove the word "not" and instead take the meaning, "I am fat." That is not what you want. To get around this, phrase your affirmation to describe what you are. "I am thin" will work. So would, "I am a healthy person." An added advantage to this is that as your mind processes this information, your conscious mind will start to be influenced by this and make you a healthier person. This is a tactic to use on bad habits you are trying to quit, such as overeating, being late, or procrastinating.

Examples:

- I have a nice smile.
- I am a good listener.
- I have a sense of humor.

Your affirmations also have to be personal. That is, they should connect with your needs, desires and goals. If you write down affirmations that you got off a website or make your affirmation common, it will escape your subconscious' notice. If you want your affirmation to stick, tie it to a goal you have. "I am a person who shows up on time for movies" is a good example. Here are more:

- I am an artist who paints four days out of every week.
- I am a cook who can prepare 10 different healthy dishes.
- I am a writer who submits a short story every month.

- I am a student who reads one new book a week.

Make sure your goal is realistic, though. If your affirmation is unrealistic, you will fail to achieve your goal, which may lead to more negative self-talk and completely cancel out the affirmation.

Keep your affirmations brief. After all, your subconscious is like a child. If you try to make your affirmation too long, your subconscious will start to ignore you, or perhaps only process part of the affirmation and give it a different meaning than you intended.

Make sure your affirmations are corrective. They should be encouraging you to make a change in your life. If your affirmations are reinforcing a belief you already have of yourself, you are not improving your self-image.

Present is another attribute. In the same way your subconscious does not realize the absence of something, it also does not realize anything except for the here and now. In a way, it is kind of a zen attitude. The past is gone, and the future has not happened yet. All that is left is the now. This is why your affirmations have to be phrased as something that is happening at this moment. You are not going to be anything, and you will not do anything. Instead, say what you are. Your subconscious mind will catch on.

Examples:
- I am a responsible student.
- I am a careful mathematician.
- I am an adventurous person.
- I am someone who loves to dance.

Finally, your affirmations must be concise. Going back to the analogy of talking to a child, you need to explain things in concrete terms for the child to understand them. If you tell a child to be positive, the child will have no idea what you mean. You will need to spell it out, telling the child he or she should smile and say hi to his or her friends when the child sees them. The same principle applies when writing your affirmations. Do you want to be self-confident? Then take time and think about what you mean when you say self-confident. Maybe that encompasses asking someone out that you find attractive. Maybe it means not being embarrassed when you ask for help. Your affirmations, then, can be, "I am a person who is confident when I ask someone out on a date" and "I feel good about myself when I ask for assistance."

Here are more concise affirmations:

- I am someone who reads classic literature, such as Dickens and Tolstoy.

- I am someone who swims 20 laps five days a week.

- I am someone who completes his or her projects the day before they are due.

How to use your affirmations

When you have written down your affirmations, review them and then pick out no more than 12 of them. At least make sure you have seven. If you cannot come up with seven instances in which you talk negatively to yourself, do what you can and congratulate yourself for being amazingly well adjusted.

Make sure the affirmations you select represent what you want. Save the rest, though. You can come back to them after you have imprinted the first set on your mind. What you are going to do with these affirmations is repeat them. Start your day by reading your affirmations and make them one of the last things you read before going to bed at night. During the day, read your affirmations. Try to look at your affirmations five or six times throughout the day. You can also write them on an index card and tape it in areas where you will be looking, such as next to your computer, in your locker, as a file on your smartphone, or as a bookmark. If your computer has a microphone, you can download free recording software at **http://sourceforge.net/projects/audacity** and make an MP3 file of you saying your affirmations. Then put it onto your MP3 player and listen to it throughout the day.

Getting these affirmations to sink into your subconscious requires days and weeks of constant repetition. So take your core group of affirmations and keep repeating them to yourself for at least a month — and not a February-sized month, even if you start in a leap year. A full 30 days is the minimum; then revisit your main list of affirmations and see if you want to add more affirmations in, take affirmations out, or even see if the current affirmations need to be revised to be brought more in line with your goals. Then go another month. Eventually, your subconscious will make these affirmations part of your self-image. Just as important, you will join the select club of people who become their own cheerleaders instead of people who constantly tear themselves down.

IS THERE NO LIMIT TO WHAT AFFIRMATIONS CAN DO?

In addition to patching up your self-esteem and boosting it to levels previously un-dreamed of, there are people who claim that affirmations can help you reach your goals — any goal. As in the "get into Harvard" goal or "make $1 million a year" goal. Is this true? That is not what this book is about. We are only going to use affirmations here as a tool to get you talking positively to yourself.

On the other hand, if you need something more to occupy your time, shooting for the moon will not hurt. So here is a quick tutorial on how to use affirmations to achieve any goal. First, select your goal. Any goal is good because this technique is supposed to work on anything. Then write down your affirmation, beginning with "I, [your name], will..." like this:

- I, Robert Layton, will get into Yale.

- I, Samantha Braxton, will have enough money to buy my own car.

Do this 15 times a day for at least six months, and you are supposed to achieve your goal, according to proponents of these type of affirmations, including Scott Adams in his book *The Dilbert Future*. The reasons for this working range from the plausible — constant repetition of a goal focuses your mind like a laser on achieving that goal and making the probability of that goal coming true much higher — to the bizarre, such as the theory that focusing your thoughts influences reality to give you what you want.

> Two bits of advice if you do conduct this experiment:
>
> 1. Do not put down, "I will get back together with my ex" as your goal. You are trying to move on.
>
> 2. If you do come into $1 million, remember who told you about this technique.

I Can See the Future

Although constant repetition is a large part of affirmations, the subconscious also responds well to a positive image. This is where the technique called **visualization** comes in. Visualization increases the rate at which your subconscious absorbs the affirmations' messages, and it works even better if you can visualize while you are relaxed. Visualization is simply envisioning yourself after you have achieved your goal. See yourself being assertive, getting your way in a discussion, and feeling good about it. See yourself balancing your checkbook on a weekly basis, confident that you are in control of your finances.

One of the best times to practice visualization is right before you go to sleep. You are already unwinding after the day's events, and you can use that time to envision what you will be doing when you achieve your goal. It is a pleasant way to fall asleep. You can also designate time each week to devote to visualization. Pick an area that makes you feel relaxed and comfortable. You might have a favorite chair, or you can stretch out on the sofa or lie down on your bed. Taking a long, hot bath is a good option, too. Then put on soft, relaxing music, start relaxing, and visualize yourself in the future. If you recorded your affirmations, you can also break out a speaker system and set your MP3 player to continually repeat your affirmations as you relax.

Visualization has an added bonus for people who are suffering from heartbreak. It offers a built-in retreat and gives you time to indulge yourself when you feel exhausted. Plus, you are not retreating or taking a break from reality when you visualize — you are confronting it and making sure you get the reality you deserve.

Keep Yourself Busy

Idle hands are the devil's playthings. Breaking up with someone creates a void in your life that your ex used to occupy. As any doctor will tell you, the more you poke at an open wound, the more you are reminded it is there. The best thing you can do is to put on a bandage and let it start to heal. In the case of a breakup, you help the wound to heal by filling it with plenty of other things to get you to take your mind off your absent ex.

One set of relationship gurus, stand-up comedian Greg Behrendt and his wife Amiira Ruotola-Behrendt, say to dive headfirst into your routine. Avoid the temptation to take a week off of school and spend it in bed or watching television. Instead, go to class and just remember that, since you are still learning, you are doing something productive. Rejoice in that feeling. While you might not love school, you can still feel good about the fact that you are accomplishing something. In addition to schoolwork, keep up your other routines. Do you get a coffee every Wednesday or go to the gym five times a week? Keep doing them. Your routines keep you going and can also be pillars of stability you can cling to in a time of stress.

It Is All About You

Outside your routines, your main criteria for keeping busy should be that it is something you want to do. Almost everyone has something they have wanted to do. Now is the time to break those dreams and goals out of storage and finally start to achieve them. Here is a list to get you started:

Goals

- Learn to speak a different language
- Learn a martial art
- Teach yourself to play guitar
- Read a book series
- Watch movies you have not gotten around to seeing

Hobbies

- Teach yourself origami
- Learn to juggle
- Take up yoga
- Collect coins or stamps
- Go ballroom dancing
- Knit
- Paint
- Write (bonus points if you write a book and submit it)
- Play video games

Other

- Clean up your desk
- Organize your closet
- Clean your room

This is about what you want to do. Although you have the same concerns about time and money that people have, you also have money you can use for your entertainment. Time to get that money out and use it. Goals, such as world travel, might take time to achieve, but planning for a long-range goal can be as rewarding as doing it, and it keeps you as busy as a hobby would.

A good strategy for keeping yourself active is to come up with two or three big hobbies or goals. You might want to mix them up. Select one long-term goal, along with hobbies, or maybe even something from the "other" category — it is all right to admit that you might have let the housekeeping go during your breakup. Then, start to figure out how to achieve it. Get yourself a sheet of paper, or even take out your journal again. Write down your three goals or hobbies, and list the next step you can take to make them happen. If you want to travel to Oslo after graduating, you might want to see when the best time is for visiting Norway. You might also want to do a quick Internet search and see what tourist attractions are in Oslo, and then buy a guidebook or a smartphone app that tells you what to do when traveling to Oslo. If you want to learn a hobby, such as origami or juggling, your first step would be doing research on the Internet. If you want to clean your room, then start listing what needs to be cleaned. From this point on, when you get stuck, go to those lists, look at the last thing you entered, and see if you have done it. Then, list the next thing that needs to be done. By doing this, you will be putting your mind in problem-solving mode and make achieving these goals and hobbies much easier.

EASY OR HARD?

When you are deciding on what you want to pursue, you might wonder whether pursuing easier or harder goals is better. After all, reading a book you have been interested in is easier than learning how to play the guitar like Jimi Hendrix. While the rule of doing what you want to do applies to this aspect of selecting your hobbies as much as any other aspect, here are one or two guidelines. If you have had your self-esteem hit badly by the breakup, you might want to go for an easy win. You might also want to do something easy if you feel so lethargic that getting out of bed is a challenge. On the other hand, if you have too much adrenaline coursing through your system or if you still dream of shaking your ex the next time you see him or her, you might want to get involved in something more difficult, giving you another target that will let you transfer all that energy for a sustained time.

Thank You

While you are keeping yourself busy, you can use gratitude lists as a way to keep yourself thinking positively about your life. Gratitude lists are like daily vitamins, and they have the same effect, contributing to your mental well-being instead of your physical well-being.

The concept is simple. All you have to do is regularly write down something for which you are thankful. Choose a time in the morning and in the evening. You might also want to schedule in time during lunch to bolster your spirits. As for the things for which you are grateful, that is up to you. In the beginning, you might want to start small. Try something basic such as, "I am thankful for my family," or "I am thankful I am not sick." These might seem like ordinary things to be thankful for, and that is the whole point. While you are still putting the pieces of your heart back together, you can use a reminder of the things that are going well in your life. This is not going to magically make your grieving go away, but it will balance out the negative thoughts.

One of the best parts of a gratitude list is that you can keep it anywhere. If you feel disorganized, write your list on sheets of scrap paper. You can also buy a small notebook to keep with you or a little leather-bound volume if you want to be artistic. This being the 21st century, you can also take out your smartphone and type your gratitude list out as a note or series of notes. Another option is to use the Internet. Post what you are feeling grateful for on your social media account, and you will be able to see your gratitude list grow and even get encouragement from your friends.

Keeping yourself together mentally provides benefits as you go through your breakup, and it also helps to lessen those feelings of wanting to just go home and slip under the covers that people experience when confronted with a stressful situation. That is a good thing because you are going to need that extra energy for the next chapter's topic — keeping yourself physically fit.

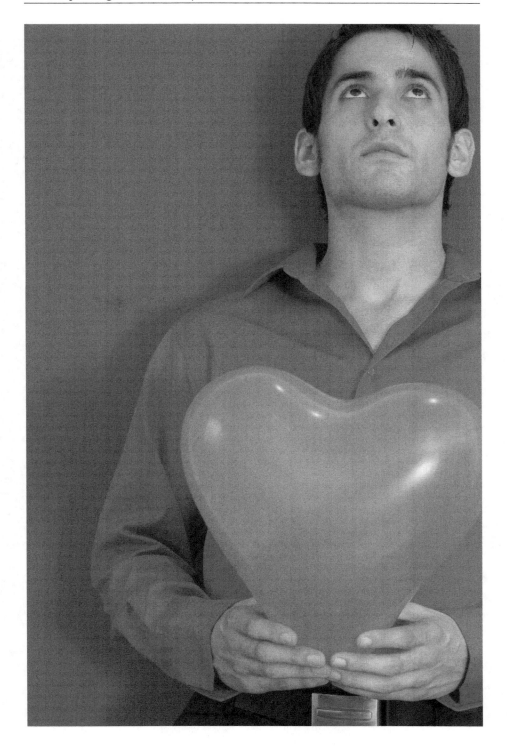

Chapter 6

How to Not Let Yourself Go Physically

Sitting around and doing nothing during the grieving process is not doing you any good. Neither is that comfort food you have been eating. Sure, it can feel good for a day or two, but after a week you might start to notice that your clothes are getting tighter on you. Even if you ignore the health issues associated with gaining weight, looking in the mirror and realizing you have put on pounds can kill your self-esteem.

Aside from the extra weight, letting yourself go physically can drag you down in other ways. Doing nothing all day does not feel rewarding, and at the end of the day you might even be feeling depressed from seeing nothing but your four walls. Being depressed saps your energy further and leaves you feeling less like doing anything than ever, and a vicious circle is created.

Keeping yourself physically fit is just as important as keeping yourself mentally fit. It might not be what you feel like doing initially, but the better you take care of your body, the more confident you will feel after you have gotten over your breakup. It will also give you one less thing to worry about during the grieving process, which will also make keeping yourself mentally fit easier.

Where Are You Starting?

Before reading about concepts, such as eating right and exercising, figure out where you stand as far as physical fitness. This will give you a baseline, and if you feel disappointed by the results, it will give you a goal to work toward and provide you with something else you can do to occupy your thoughts as you get through your breakup. First, determine your current level of activity. What do you do for exercise during the week? Do you go to a gym, swim at a pool, or go for an occasional run? Do you spend time during the day on your feet or walking? Or is the physical part of your day when you walk to class?

Second, consider your eating habits. Do you eat out? How much space do snack foods take up in your cupboards? What do you do for dinner?

Last, record your body mass index, or BMI. This number gives you a better sense of where you stand physically than just your weight. Although you might want a calculator, the formula for calculating your BMI is easy.

First, multiply your weight in pounds by 0.45.

Second, convert your height to inches. Then multiply that number by 0.0254 and square the result.

Last, divide the first number by the second. The resulting number is your BMI.

The formula looks like this:

$$\frac{(weight)x.0.45}{[(height)x0.0254]^2}$$

Example: A man who weighs 195 pounds and is 5-feet-9-inches wants to know his BMI. First, he multiplies his weight by 0.45 and gets a result of 87.75. He then converts his height into inches, getting a result of 69. He multiplies 69 by 0.0254 and gets a result of 1.75. Squaring that results in 3.07. Last, he divides 87.75 by 3.07 for a BMI of 28.58.

Then, compare your BMI number against the chart below, according to the Mayo Clinic:

If your result is 18.5 or below, you are considered underweight.

If your result is between the numbers of 18.5 and 24.9, you are at a healthy weight.

If your result is between the numbers of 25 and 29.9, you are considered overweight.

If your result is 30 or above, you are considered obese.

In the example above, the subject's BMI of 28.58 puts him in the overweight category.

If you have access to the Internet, you can locate a BMI calculator. Try the one at the website of the National Heart Lung and Blood Institute at **www.nhlbi.nih.gov/health/educational/lose_wt/ BMI/bmicalc.htm**.

Take a deep breath

After going through that quick self-assessment, your self-esteem might be dropping like a stone in a mine shaft. Before you start to panic, take a deep breath and relax. Do not worry — whatever results you got, your secret is safe. The goal here is not to motivate you to achieve that near-unhealthy level of thin reserved for supermodels, and you do not have to feel bad about your weight or exercise level. This is designed to help you get through a breakup. If you can come out the other end more fit than you did when you started, you will be able to feel more self-confident and happier with yourself and can also turn the negative of heartbreak into a positive.

Commit to Improve Yourself

Once you know where you stand physically, make a commitment to improve. If you are already in good standing physically, you can take time to reaffirm your commitment to being physically fit.

According to the Mayo Clinic, it takes several steps to be healthier. The first is to become more active. You do not have to run out and join a gym or start training for a marathon, but instead just schedule a half-hour into your day where you can do a low-intensity exercise, such as walking. If your schedule is too hectic to make room for exercise every day, you can get the same benefits by scheduling a longer exercise session over fewer days. For instance, you can put in 45-minute exercise sessions for five days out of the week, or you can exercise only three days a week if you increase your exercise session time to one hour. Three hours in one day is not going to work.

Another step to take on the path to healthier living is to be realistic about what you want to achieve. If you weigh more than 200 pounds, you are going to be disappointed if you try to slim down to below 130 in the course of two months. Instead, accept that losing weight is more like a marathon than a sprint, and your attempts to be more physically fit will go better if you lose weight at a slow and steady pace. According to doctors, the safe rate to lose weight is one to two pounds per week.

Setting realistic goals will also help you to boost your self-confidence, which is another necessary component of living healthier. If you do not feel you are making any progress when you work out, why will you continue to go? Experiment and try new things when you are exercising, such as varying the exercises you do, changing the routes you take when you go running or walking, or seeing if you look forward to exercising more when you have a friend with whom you can work out. You can also ask veteran gym members if they have any motivational secrets that make them work out as regularly as they do.

Last, the big thing to do to live healthier is to make a permanent change to your lifestyle. Living healthier is not something that happens overnight. Instead, it is a commitment you make every day. As time goes by, you might notice that you are living healthier, and that instead of reaching for a soda when you are thirsty, you grab an iced tea instead. Living healthier is also a process, which means you will have more successes one day than another, and if you eat too much junk food, the correct response is to acknowledge your mistake and try again instead of giving up.

Take a Trip to See the Food Pyramid

The first step in being more physically fit is to eat right. Not caring about what you eat is a way of life for people, and you are used to obeying your body's orders when it comes to food. Need a pizza? Eat a pizza. Want a salad? Eat a salad. Although that theory has its own pitfalls, during a breakup your body behaves differently than normal. People feel too sick to eat anything. For others, their body tells them to keep eating to appease the bottomless feeling in their stomachs. Neither extreme produces good results. Eating right will give your body the nutrients it needs and keep you feeling full without gorging yourself on calories.

The biggest problem is determining the best guide to eating healthy. While there are guides out there, one of the best comes from the Mayo Clinic. It presents the Mayo Clinic's own version of the Food and Drug Administration's Food Pyramid, which is a refined version of the four food groups:

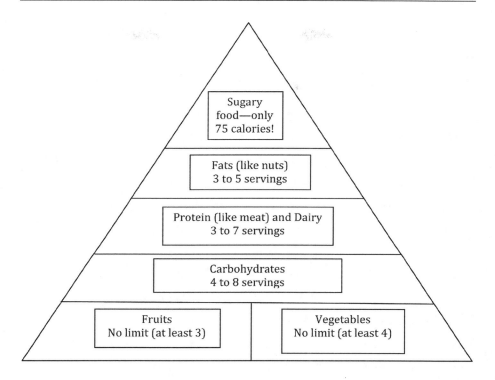

Now that you have a guide, the next question becomes, how many calories can you have? As a rule, you will need to consume 2,000 calories per day. If you want to weigh less, consume fewer calories. The Mayo Clinic again offers guidelines. Women who weigh more than 300 pounds should reduce their calorie intake to 1,600 per day. Women weighing less than 300 pounds but more than 250 should eat 1,400 daily calories, while women who weigh less than 250 pounds should eat 1,200 calories per day.

For men, if you weigh more than 300 pounds, the Mayo Clinic recommends decreasing your daily calories to 1,800 if you want to lose weight. Men weighing more than 250 pounds but less than 300 should consume 1,600 calories, and men weighing under 250 should eat 1,400 daily calories.

These are only beginning suggestions. If you feel extremely hungry throughout the day and you are following a balanced diet, then add 200 calories to your diet. Try not to exceed 2,000 calories, though.

What if you are happy with your current weight and only want to maintain it? The best way to do so is with a calorie calculator. Ideally, you will be able to talk to a dietician to get an accurate number of the calories you can have per day. If you cannot get to a dietician, however, you can go online to find a calorie per day calculator. An easy-to-use calorie calculator is available at **http://walking.about.com/cs/calories/l/blcalcalc.htm**. Another good one is located at: **http://dietforum.com/calories-per-day.htm**. These calculators, however, might give you different answers when you put in the same numbers. You might want to use the average of these numbers instead of relying on just one.

WHAT IS A CALORIE?

When talking about calories, if you eat too many, you gain weight, and if you burn more than you lose, you get thinner. But what is a calorie?

A calorie is a unit of measurement that is used to measure energy. The actual definition of a calorie is the amount of energy needed in the form of heat, to raise the temperature of a gram of water by 1 degree Celsius, or 1.8 degrees Fahrenheit. However, calories today are kilocalories, or the amount of energy needed to raise the temperature of a kilogram of water by 1 degree Celsius.

So how does this have anything to do with a person's diet? Human beings burn energy all the time. Each heartbeat burns a bit of energy, as does every other kind of muscle movement. They need a source for all this energy, and it comes in the form of food. So the number of calories a food has is a measure of the potential energy it will give the body.

The principle of a diet is that if you lower the amount of calories coming in, your body is not getting the necessary potential energy it needs to function. It has to siphon that energy from somewhere to survive, and it finds that energy in the stores of fat it has saved up.

One serving is how much?

To eat right, you will have to take a methodical approach to food. Break out your measuring spoons and cups, and prepare to get them dirty. As you are aware, packaged foods have nutritional information printed on the side, including the number of calories per serving. What you might not know, though, is what companies consider a serving to be. For instance, if you look at the back of a container of oatmeal, one serving consists of a half of a cup. If you have access to a measuring cup, look at how much a half-cup holds. You are going to be surprised, if only because cereal bowls can easily hold four times that amount.

Eating healthily means watching your portion sizes, and this is something that can give people trouble. Portion size is common sense. With fruits, for instance, one apple counts as one serving of fruit. So does one orange. One slice of bread counts as a serving of grains. On the other end of the spectrum, three ounces of fish or shrimp count as one serving. So do three ounces of chicken or turkey. Then there are the miniature amounts of food that qualify as a serving of fats, such as seven almonds or a teaspoon of oil.

Out of these portions, the one that gives people trouble trying to figure out how to measure three ounces of chicken, turkey, fish, or shrimp. There is a simple rule of thumb to let you know the amount of meat to get in a serving — your serving of meat should be the size of a standard deck of playing cards. So keep a deck of cards somewhere in your kitchen the next time you are serving yourself.

Get Moving

Exercise also plays a huge role in being fit. Again, you do not need to enroll in a gym or buy a home workout station to get the advantages of exercising. Setting aside 30 minutes a day for light exercise works just as well.

When you exercise, choose something you will enjoy. If you think walking is not challenging enough, try jogging. If you want to focus more on strength training, lift weights. If you like swimming, see if there is a pool near you where you can swim laps. You might even see if there is a yoga class or a martial arts course offered nearby.

During the first times you exercise, start off slow. You do not want to discourage yourself. Then, after you have gotten into the habit of exercising, start to make the exercise more challenging. Add five more minutes to your walking time, for instance, or reduce the breaks you take while out jogging. When lifting weights, add 2 to 5 more pounds onto the amounts you started with, or add another set of lifting weights. If swimming is your exercise of choice, swim more laps the next time you are in the pool. Before you know it, you will have developed a workout schedule.

Feeling Good

When you exercise, your body produces endorphins. The hypothalamus and pituitary gland produce these chemicals in your brain. They are the body's all-natural painkillers. Endorphins in your mind produce a sense of well-being and a euphoric feeling that can cover up the pain your body feels. These endorphins are effective at combating negative feelings, such as sadness and anger.

Do you have to push your body to its ultimate limits to get the effects of endorphins? No. You can get the same benefits from endorphins when jogging as you can when you do heavy lifting in the gym. If you push yourself to exercise too hard and for too long, you might injure yourself. Moderation when exercising is less risky, and you are more likely to stick with a moderate exercise schedule than with an intense regimen.

Can you take it?

Before you throw yourself into a workout, you might want to get a physical checkup first. While going to the doctor's office is rarely fun, it is a good way to make sure that no latent health problems will be getting in your way while you exercise. You have enough on your mind already. You do not need to deal with anything else — especially a hospital stay.

People treat a physical checkup the same way other people treat having a housekeeper clean their apartment — making sure the awful messes are hidden from sight. Avoid that urge. Bring up any health problems or concerns you might have with your doctor. Although you might feel embarrassed to bring up these concerns, you will get more benefit out of the checkup if you do.

When you get a checkup, tell the doctor why you are there, and ask his or her for any advice he or she might have about setting up an exercise schedule and any advice he or she has on easing yourself into an exercise routine. Do this and you will have one less worry on your mind as you start exercising regularly.

Date Night: Not Just for Couples

During your slow and steady path to rebuild or maintain your physical health, resolve to take one evening out of your schedule and devote it to doing whatever you want. Couples schedule regular date nights to have alone time and do something fun with someone they value. Your date nights are the same, and even better, the person you will end up appreciating more is yourself.

The first step to a successful date night is getting rid of any outside interruptions. Turn off your cellphone, for starters. Then shutdown your computer. Whatever time you decide on, there is only one rule — make it consistent. If you stay up late on Tuesday nights, make sure you can have your date night every Tuesday. Over time, it will be a ritual you can look forward to doing, and it will give you a reason to look forward to a day in the week that is overlooked.

While you can work in the hobbies and crafts you are trying into your date night, you can also spend your time relaxing. When was the last time you had time to yourself to guarantee you could go shopping? What about the last time you could sit down and go through your book collection? What about the last time you cooked something tasty for yourself? Indulge; it does not even have to involve spending money. Perhaps you have a TV show you enjoy watching. On your date night, pop popcorn and watch the show with no interruptions. Watching TV is something you might do every evening, but do you get to indulge in your love for a show?

Over time, you might want to expand on the activities you do for your date night, or you might want to develop a new routine entirely. During the spring and summer, doing an activity that takes advantage of the nice weather, such as bike riding or playing a round of Frisbee golf, is a wonderful idea. In the winter, however, you might want to find a more indoors-related activity, such as taking a painting class, or watching movies.

Spending time with yourself has its benefits. By indulging in something you want to do, you are giving your subconscious the message that your desires are worth listening to and acting on. Setting up a regular date night is also proof that you value yourself, and while you might have to satisfy other people's needs while you are working, there is one night a week where your needs come first.

Other Ways to Take Care of Yourself

Being healthy is not just about eating the right foods or being active. When you go through a breakup, make sure to maintain areas of your life you might not have considered before.

One of those areas is sleeping. On average, a teenager needs at least seven hours of sleep per night, with the optimal amount being closer to nine hours. A study the University of Warwick did in 2010 showed that if someone does not get at least six hours of sleep per night, he or she was 12 percent more likely to suffer an early death, as opposed to people who manage to get enough sleep at night. Fortunately, the study found that sleeping more than eight hours a night did not directly affect one's chances of dying early, but it did point out that excessive sleep might be the result of a mental disorder or a serious disease. Set up a regular bedtime at night, and if you find that you cannot get to sleep, set up an appointment with your doctor.

Also, abstain from drinking and recreational drug use, especially after you have broken up with someone. The main problem with using alcohol and drugs , such as marijuana, during a breakup is that being under their effects feels better than coping with your grief. Using drugs and alcohol to avoid having to deal with your grief puts you at serious risk for becoming addicted.

People think of reinventing your look as something that only happens at a beauty salon or in an expensive department store, but that does not have to be the case. For instance, you can just get a different kind of haircut or pick up a new pair of shoes or a stylish jacket. This shows that you are not the same person you were before the breakup. Reinventing your look will also give you a needed confidence boost when you look in the mirror and see a new, confident person staring back at you.

Keeping yourself physically healthy is an ongoing process, and it is a way to keep yourself occupied as you get over your breakup. At one point, you will wake up and realize that you do not miss your ex and that you look good, too.

Chapter 7

Getting Support From Others

N o matter what your heartbreak is like, another person can make it easier. Having even one friend around who will listen to your complaints and help to get you interacting with the rest of the world is a valuable asset, and having a support group can ease the burden you feel.

Pride in the Name of Heartbreak

The first hurdle of getting a friend to help you is admitting you need help. This can be hard to overcome. After all, you already feel humiliated from the breakup. Admitting you cannot cope with it on your own seems like adding insult to injury. Or, you might be the kind of person who hates burdening others with your problems. These sentiments are understandable, but —

your friends are your friends because they are there for you. They are not going to feel inconvenienced because you call them to talk about missing your ex. Friends feel honored if you trust them enough to discuss your problems with them. A friend will know that you are not doing well and ask if he or she can help you. In that case, all you have to do is open up.

If you do not have a friend who preemptively asks if he or she can help and you are wondering how to select a friend to turn to, here is a helpful list of qualities to look for.

First, the friend you choose should know about your relation-ship and how it ended. This is not the time to reconnect with the people you knew in elementary school and start explaining that you feel bad you have had your heart broken. On a similar note, your friend should ideally have experienced a breakup himself or herself. If he or she has, your friend will understand what you are going through and will be more sympathetic.

Ease of communication is a big factor in determining whether you can trust someone to help you through a breakup. Make sure your friend can be easily reached, so you are not left with having to suffer through a lonely evening before your friend gets back to you the next day. You might also want to make sure your friend lives nearby, so you can hang out together when you are feeling lonely or depressed. Also, ask your friend if he or she can set aside time every day so you can talk if you need to. He or she does not have to put his or her life on hold during that time, but you can make sure that from 7 to 8 p.m., your friend will have his or her cellphone on or will have a messaging program running.

Make sure that whomever you choose to help you through a breakup is a good listener. You might be grateful for any advice you receive during this time, but unless your friend listens to what you have to say, the advice will not do you any good. Last, make sure your friend is someone who thinks you are a decent person. During a breakup you want someone who is going to listen and be supportive of you, not someone who feels the best way to support you is to help you fix all those imperfections he or she has observed.

WHAT IF SOMEONE ASKS YOU TO HELP GET HIM OR HER THROUGH A BREAKUP?

You know how to select someone to help you get through your breakup, but what do you do when one of your friends asks you to help him get over a breakup? First, feel good about yourself. It says something about you as a friend and as a person that your friend trusts you to get him through a difficult time. Just do not let that feeling go to your head. The larger one's ego, the more difficult helping someone else becomes.

When you take on the responsibility of helping a friend get through a breakup, keep in mind simple guidelines. Your friend is not expecting you to help fix him. While your friend is crying into his pillow and asking what he did wrong, you might be tempted to answer. Avoid this temptation. Your friend's self-esteem is already tanking, and you do not want to add to it. Instead, just listen and be there for your friend. If he asks you what he did wrong, tell him that people can be wrong for each other, and the fact that your friend broke up with his ex does not reflect on your friend as a person.

There are exceptions to this rule. If your friend is an addict or abused his ex, gently suggest that he get professional help. Even then, do not take responsibility for fixing your friend. You are here to support.

Share your experiences with your friend. You can draw on your own breakups and tell your friend there is light at the end of the tunnel, even after that pesky freight train has finished running him over. Talk about what you did to get through your breakup, and make suggestions for your friend. According to relationship gurus — and husband and wife team — Greg Behrendt and Amiira Ruotola-Behrendt, just hearing that someone else went through the same situation can be a huge source of comfort.

As you are sharing your experiences, make things fun. This is going to have to be your responsibility, so when your friend needs to talk about how lonely he feels when he goes to a movie without an ex, schedule a session of Frisbee golf or a walk through the park. Doing this will help to occupy your friend's mind and show him that the world goes on and there is still fun to be had.

When helping a friend get through a breakup, be patient. Getting over heartbreak takes time and happens gradually, so do not expect your friend to tell you he is over his ex. This is a long-term project, but it will pay off. However, make sure you do not sacrifice your personal life to help your friend. You can set boundaries on your personal life without being a bad person. If you cannot talk to your friend while at sports practice, let him know that. If you have extracurricular activities on certain days, let your friend know when they are; you can also invite him to join. Just make sure you set up a plan so you can be there for your friend when he needs to talk.

Good luck — you got through your breakup. So can your friend.

With a Little Help From Your Friends — and Family

Fortunately, you will have friends who are willing to help as you go through your breakup. You will have the support of your family, too. Having multiple friends to support you gives you more advantages, as opposed to relying on just one friend. For instance, you have more options available if you need someone to talk to. You also have a better chance of being able to hang out with someone if the first friend you call is unavailable. Last, by having a support system of friends, you have a better chance of finding someone to do an activity you want to do. If you feel that what you need to heal is to go for a run, get a friend who also likes to exercise. If your exercising friend does not like science fiction and you want to check out that new sci-fi movie, call up a friend who likes those movies. If you just want to go to the mall and shop, select a friend who is an avid shopper. Having several friends also means you can do several activities that are more fun with more people there.

Good group activities:

- Go to the beach
- Play Frisbee
- Have a snowball fight
- Play multiplayer video games
- Play a sport, such as volleyball or football
- Go to a movie
- Walk around a festival
- Go out to dinner

Family can help

Even with the support your friends give, there is nothing like being able to talk to your parents. Being able to talk to your mother or father is therapeutic, no matter how old you are. No one can love you unconditionally like your mom and your dad. Plus, who else knows you better? Brothers and sisters can be another good source of support, and close sibling relationships can be as beneficial as having a best friend around. A sibling can also support you in ways that you might be hesitant to ask of your friends, such as taking a 1 a.m. phone call to discuss what a jerk your last boyfriend or girlfriend was.

PARENT SUBSTITUTES

Not everyone has a close relationship with their parents. If you happen to fall into this category, do not worry — you likely have someone with whom you have a parent-like relationship. These can include relatives, such as an aunt, uncle, grandparent, or even an older cousin. You can also have a parent-like relationship with someone who is not related to you, such as your best friend's mother.

CASE STUDY: HOW TO LIVE THROUGH A ROUGH BREAKUP

Megan Holt is a personal trainer and grad student. Expect good things from her.

When Megan broke up with her boyfriend, she started a new job within a week and moved from Michigan to New York City. The only problem was, her ex was living in New York.

"[My ex] started talking to me again because I was close to him proximity-wise," Megan says. The fact that they had the same friends also meant that she would occasionally see her ex. "I ignored him or was reserved with him," she recalls.

Then her ex threatened her. "That's when I told him if he didn't knock it off, I'd call the cops on him," she says.

What helped Megan get over her breakup were her friends and her family. "I got more help from them than I ever expected," she says. "They are the reason I am still here today. They were there during the late-night, tear-filled phone calls, the depression, and they have stuck by me and encouraged me as I've rebuilt my life in a better, stronger way."

Megan also changed "nearly everything" in her life. She went out with a new group of friends and began new hobbies, such as drawing, painting and triathlons.

Still, the breakup has altered Megan's attitude toward dating. "I do not want to hurt that bad again," she states. "I have been working to overcome [that fear] by taking things slow and not letting myself get over-invested. I have yet to get into a relationship that is as serious since the breakup and, should I find myself considering it, the guy will have to stand up to multiple interrogations from family and friends." Megan has broken up with other people since her bout of heartbreak, but she says they were "far easier."

As a result of her experience, Megan has a set of standards she will not compromise on. Nothing too specific, but he has to have read more than five books in the past decade, for instance. She also has advice on how to get over heartbreak. "Don't try to stay friends — bad idea," Megan says. "It does not work. Give yourself time and distance, emotionally and physically, to heal. If, in a few years, you feel ready, then maybe give being friends a shot, but don't bank on it happening.

"Take up a healthy new hobby instead of self-medicating with drugs or alcohol — that ends poorly. Talk to your friends and family, and don't be afraid to cry on their shoulders. They'll be there for you."

Social therapy

When you are in a relationship, you talk less with your old friends as you spend more time and become more attached to your partner. This is good while the relationship is working. Unfortunately, after a breakup you might feel your selection of friends is limited, or worse, you only know your friends because your ex was friends with them first. If you find yourself in this situation, do not despair. If you used to hang out with anyone in the area, now is the time to contact them again. Tell them what is going on with minimum dramatics and ask if you can hang out with them again. The odds are good they will say yes.

If you like video games, you have even more options available. Current video game systems have an Internet connection with online areas where you can talk with friends if they are online. You might also find your friends online in massive multiplayer online role-playing games. People consider running around killing monsters to be a therapeutic way of dealing with bad feelings, even if the American Psychiatric Association has not formally recognized it.

Getting Professional Help

There might come a time where you realize you are not dealing well with your breakup. It might be a subtle sign, such as still missing your ex. Other times the signs might be more obvious — for instance, if you do not have the energy to get out of bed or you have no optimism anymore. If you feel you need more help than your friends and family can provide, you might want to take to your parents about seeing a psychologist.

Seeing a therapist is not a prospect that thrills people. To admit that you might need professional help in getting through your breakup can seem less appealing than admitting you need help from your friends, but a good therapist can help you in ways your friends might not. First, you can tell your therapist things you might be hesitant to talk about with your friends, such as the intimate details of your relationship with your ex. It can be easier to share more personal information with someone you do not know rather than your close friends, and someone on the outside can offer better advice than those who are close to the situation. A therapist can give you guidance, make suggestions as to how to heal and work with you to help you get over your heartbreak. You will also discover that since your therapist wants you to get well, he or she will be one of your biggest supporters. There is no shame in seeking professional help.

When you decide you want to see a therapist, take time beforehand to do research. Talk to your family and do a quick search online to locate the therapists in your area. If you live in a rural area, you might have to widen the range of your search to include the towns near you. Once you have a list of therapists, start calling them. Find out what kind of therapy they specialize in because while it might be best to find a therapist who specializes in teens, you might not be looking for a therapist whose specialty is helping patients overcome abuse or trauma, unless your relationship was extremely bad. Other factors to take into consideration are:

- What are the therapist's hours?

- How does the therapist feel about medication?

- Is the therapist covered by your health care plan?

ASK ANGIE

One Internet resource that people have found useful is Angie's List. This website invites consumers to rate contractors, from carpenters to landscapers. Health care specialists are also covered, and you might find reviews on potential therapists by searching the website at **www.angieslist.com**.

Once you have investigated the therapists, meet them in person. Have your parents schedule an interview with each therapist so you can get a sense of whether you are at ease with them. If you do not understand a term they use, ask them to define it. Last, once you have decided on a therapist, schedule an appointment. On your first visit you will have to fill out forms and discuss the reason for wanting to visit a therapist, so schedule extra time for that. If you can, fill out the forms beforehand.

When you visit a therapist, think about what you want to talk about beforehand. Your therapist might instruct you to keep a journal of your thoughts for this purpose. He or she might even suggest things for you to consider between visits. While you might be hesitant to open up to a therapist at first, he is trying to help you. Consider the therapist as a new friend.

CASE STUDY: THE BENEFITS OF THERAPY

Dr. Talia Witkowski is a woman who knows how beneficial therapy can be for people who have had their hearts broken.

"I went through a breakup close to four years ago that almost killed me," she says. "I was in such emotional pain over the situation that I started getting back into the addictions I had sworn off in college. I spoke to everyone I could about the pain, but the more I spoke about the pain without finding any solution, the more heartache and pain I felt. I thought the only way I was going to overcome the obsession was to get the man back and propose marriage."

During this time in her life, she was introduced to Roy Nelson, a therapist. "I met him through introducing him to a patient I was treating for bulimia," she says. "The patient's mother knew of his services and asked me to make the introduction. I am so thankful that she did."

The therapy she received proved to be quite beneficial. "I spoke to him briefly about the pain of the breakup after the session with my client," Talia recalls. "When I did, the pain that I had been nursing for six months disappeared."

As time passed, Talia's relationship with Roy continued to bear fruit. "Through Roy's mentorship, I lost 60 pounds. I lost the cravings for unhealthy foods, alcohol, pot, and unhealthy relationships."

One of the reasons Talia's therapist was successful was because of his ability to "crack that hard doctor shell," as she puts it. "It was a gift," she says.

"My life is completely changed on account of this special [mentor]," Talia says.

Group therapy: A primer

When people think of therapists, they think of a psychiatrist's couch, talking about their dreams while the therapist sits next to them, busy taking notes. Although this type of therapy still takes place, therapists use several different types of therapy to heal their clients. One in specific that is often common for teenagers is group therapy. Group therapy depends on the personal interaction found in groups to treat the patient. Interpersonal relationships are explored, and one-on-one therapies might be used. It can potentially be more effective than one-on-one therapy. Examples of group therapy are support groups and anger management groups.

GROUP THERAPY? ME?

Group therapy is rarely portrayed as a positive experience, which is a shame because it offers benefits. One of the biggest is feeling a sense of belonging. If you are having trouble dealing with your heartbreak, knowing that there are other people out there who are struggling to overcome their grief can make you feel less alone. Group therapy also opens you up to people with different backgrounds than you and offers each participant different ways to look at a similar problem each member of the group has. By listening to what other people with similar problems have to say, you might discover something that will help you cope better with your issues. Group therapy allows you to try out new behaviors in a safe environment where people can give you feedback.

How to get the most out of therapy

No matter what type of therapy you choose, there are certain guidelines that will ensure you get the most from your treatment.

When you are in therapy, one of the best things to do is be open with your therapist. Your therapy sessions are confidential and fall under the doctor-patient confidentiality privilege. You might be embarrassed at first, but this is not the time to leave anything out. The more information your therapist has to work with, the better he or she will be able to help you. If you still feel reluctant, consider this — you know you need help, and so does your therapist; otherwise, you would not be at a therapy session. This honesty includes telling your therapist about ideas you have that you feel are irrational and conflicting or about thoughts you have that disturb you, such as thoughts of suicide or violence against your ex. You might have to uncover difficult areas of your psyche to benefit from the therapy, but you might find that something you have been embarrassed about for years is not as bad as you thought it was.

During the therapy session, your therapist will offer you pieces of advice. Do not just follow his or her advice blindly. Consider it and see if it makes sense to you, and if it does not, let your therapist know. Feedback is a vital part of psychotherapy because it is the only way for your therapist to know if the treatment is having any effect. When you offer feedback, be honest, although that does not mean you have to be rude or unkind. Your therapist will take your feedback into account, although he or she might ask that you follow his or her advice anyway. Therapy involves discomfort, and your therapist has a good reason for his or her suggestions.

Another important guideline is to follow the advice you get and apply it. If your therapist tells you, for instance, to keep a journal of your dreams for a week, do it. This will be applying the therapy to your regular life, which will be more effective than confining the therapy to your sessions. You will be able to discover whether the treatment is helping, and you can use the experience to give more feedback to the therapist, who can then use that information to make the therapy more effective. You are the one responsible for how well the therapy works. Your therapist will have explanations for your behavior and can offer you solutions, but unlike traditional medicine, the only person who can implement these cures is you.

When to end?

One common concern people have with starting therapy is whether they will be able to leave. After all, there is a common stereotype of people being in therapy for years, even decades. This is understandable. After all, as you talk with your therapist, you will establish emotional bonds with him or her, and people are hesitant to sever these bonds, especially with someone who has acted as a confidant for your problems. However, ending therapy is different for each person because each person comes into therapy with different problems and goals they work out individually with the psychologist. One patient might need therapy to overcome a fear of dating again because he cannot stop thinking about how hurt his last relationship left him. Another patient might need to work out the anger she feels at a partner who cheated on her. After time has passed, the therapist and patient will talk about how the patient has progressed, and if the patient and therapist agree that the patient has met his or her goals, they can choose to end the therapy sessions.

However, outside forces might end your therapy. Health care plans or your family's finances might prevent you from attending regular therapy sessions. In cases like these, your therapist will determine what can be done with the amount of sessions you do have. He or she might not be able to completely heal you in that event, but he or she can at least set you on the right path.

Chapter 8

Taking Stock of Your Life and Setting Goals

In the middle of your breakup, as waves of anger and depression have subsided and you are left alone with your thoughts, you will ask yourself exactly what you are doing with your life. If you are like most people who have had their heart broken, the answer is,, "I have no idea." Even goal-driven, Type A people are prone to feeling a lack of direction in their lives when their relationships end. It is understandable. After all, when a relationship ends, you need time to process who you are without your ex, and people place their identity into their romantic relationships.

One is Not the Loneliest Number

When a relationship ends, one thing that haunts newly minted singles is the question of whether they will find anyone again, or whether they will live alone. If you have had these thoughts, you know what they are like — nightmares of being the fifth wheel at parties, going to movies alone and watching as your friends pair off with other people — eventually leaving you alone, until it seems your only option is to become a recluse. Owning a house full of cats is an option.

The paradox of being mentally ready to date again is that you need to accept that being single is all right. If you feel that being alone is a curse that needs to be ended as soon as possible, you could end up falling into a trap. At worst, you might date someone who takes advantage of your desire to be with someone and uses you. You might also drive off potential dates because your desperation overshadows your good points. You might date someone who is just as desperate not to be alone, leaving the two of you in the less-than-optimal position of clinging to each other.

On the other hand, if you are comfortable being by yourself, you are not coming across as desperate. More important, you can evaluate people you might like to go out with on their merits, not simply being satisfied because they agreed to date you. The more content you are on your own, the better your chances at finding someone to date.

SO MUCH FOR THE HAPPY ENDING

Everyone wants a happy ending, and a common happy ending is at the end of a movie or the series finale of a TV show where the guy and the girl end up together. They do not get married all the time, but it happens enough that when the hero and heroine kiss, you feel sure that they will live happily forever after together.

The problem is that for all these TV shows and movies, the story ends when the script says it does. In the real world, the story keeps going after the cameras stop rolling. The ending is not necessarily happy.

If you still do not accept that being alone is just as good as being with someone else, you are not alone. There are two big rebuttals people bring up when they are told they do not need a significant other in their lives. The first is that being alone is lonely. When people talk about being single, they talk about how boring things are without anyone else around and the loneliness.

As far as boredom goes, it is a self-imposed condition. There are things to do on your own. Here are a few tips:

- Read
- Go for a walk or jog
- Exercise
- Swim
- Do crossword puzzles
- Browse the Internet
- Play video games

- Cook
- Watch a DVD
- Write
- Draw
- Knit
- Take a dance lesson

Come up with some more activities on your own. While you are single, this is a time for you to improve yourself or try new things. Granted, you can get a decent video game system and kill boredom with one game, which is also fun. You can also call up your friends, the ones who have patiently helped get you through your breakup, and do things with them. Organizing a movie night is a way to get people to hangout. So is a game night. These are also good incentives for cleaning your room, which helps to eliminate boredom with the added benefit of providing you with a feeling of productivity. You should also make it a point to get out of the house. Meet some friends for coffee, or go for a walk with them.

Be aware that being alone gives you a freedom that people in relationships do not have. Sure, you can laugh bitterly about that advantage, but consider this: When you are single, you can do almost anything you want. So eat out. Buy a movie. Plan a vacation with family. You do not have to wait for someone else to approve your actions, so enjoy this time and take full advantage of it. If your ex hated short haircuts, get a stylish new bob and see how it looks. The only thing limiting your choices is yourself.

The second big protest is that, if you are single, you need someone to feel complete, but this is not true. You have gotten through several life experiences on your own, including passing classes, getting a drivers license and figuring out what hobbies you like. These are things you have done for yourself. So ask yourself what having someone else is going to do that you cannot do yourself.

If you agreed with the above statement, you did not mean that you literally needed someone else. You meant something more along the lines of, "I want to share my life with someone and feel loved." This takes you back to the original question: How can someone love you if you do not love yourself? At a garage sale, you get a good bargain on items the owners do not value. Love works in much the same way.

Still not convinced? Try this exercise: Take out the journal you were keeping, and write down everything you like about being single. Do this every day for the next week. Even if the list starts small, as the week goes by, you will be able to add more items to the list.

CASE STUDY: DO NOT LET THE PAST SABOTAGE THE FUTURE

Russell Friedman is Executive Director of the Grief Recovery Institute (**www.griefrecoverymethod.com**) *and co-author of* The Grief Recovery Handbook, When Children Grieve, *and* Moving On.

We started with a rather commanding tone in the title of this essay. We said you will sabotage your future, not that you might sabotage your future, if you do not complete your romantic past.

The divorce rate that hovers around 50 percent only represents the endings of romantic relationships that marriage formalized. It does not include other romantic endings that cannot be counted. If there was an accurate account of divorces and the non-marriage break ups, the rate would be closer to at least 60 percent.

There are two common denominators in most breakups. One is the hidden fact that either or both members of the couple were incomplete in their prior romantic relationships. That means that either or both were dragging the unfinished emotional business from the old relationships into the new one.

The second is that people bypass their gut feelings and date people who they know are not right for them. As many as 80 percent of the people we have interacted with after their breakup tell us they knew the relationship was destined to fail, but they overrode their intuition and became a couple.

How does this happen, given that most couples embark on their new love relationships with the best of intentions? Almost all the individuals in a new relationship make a conscious decision to avoid the mistakes and pitfalls of their prior relationships.

It is wonderful to have the goal of not repeating your past, but it is another thing to accomplish that objective. Like affirmations, goals do not hold up in a crisis. You can say, "I'm magnificent and my world is filled with abundance" a million times a day, but the moment there is a crisis, you will go back to thinking you are not enough and there is no love for you, if that is your default setting.

Faced with a stimulus, which might take the form of an argument with your new mate, you will unconsciously go back to old ideas that are part of what caused your prior breakup. Your reactions will be based on old thoughts and feelings about yourself that are not true.

Those thoughts and feelings will provoke old behaviors that did not work before and still do not work.

And many of your old beliefs and behaviors relate to non-romantic relationships from earlier in life, with parents, siblings and others. The bottom line is that many of us are dragging a boatload of emotional baggage that we define as "unresolved grief."

One of the biggest myths that affect us in our reaction to grief is that time heals all wounds. But time cannot resolve what is emotionally incomplete in your romantic past, nor can your love for someone or their love for you.

"Unresolved grief drains energy and robs choice" is a phrase that appears in our book, *Moving On — Dump Your Relationship Baggage and Make Room for the Love of Your Life*.

The truth of that quote is observable in the people we have met who have been affected by a breakup and do not know how to complete what the end of the relationship has left emotionally unfinished in its wake.

"You have to let go and move on" is bad guidance. "Let go of what and move on where, and by the way, how do I do that?" Those are the questions the griever might ask that are not addressed in "letting go."

There might be a variety of techniques that will guide you with specific actions to help you discover and complete what is unfinished for you so you can recapture your energy and restart your life. But the only method we can recommend are the ones we developed in our book, *Moving On*.

Get to work immediately to discover and complete what is unfinished for you. Good, long-lasting relationships are made up of joining two whole people, not two damaged halves

Take Stock of Your Relationship

Throughout the process of piecing your heart back together, one of your goals has been to not think of your ex and try to move on, which works about as well as when someone tells you not to think of pink elephants. After you begin to get over your relationship, though, you will want to reflect on your relationship to figure out why it did not work. Trying to figure out that answer when you have first broken up is like rubbing salt in a wound. The conclusions it leads to can also be inaccurate. You might idealize the relationship and walk away with the commitment to become exactly the kind of person your ex wanted, or you might go the opposite direction and think the big mistake you made was getting involved with your ex in the first place. Once you put emotional distance between yourself and the heartbreak, though, you can get a clearer picture of what worked in the relationship and what did not work. This is important, because you can use that information to make your next relationship better.

It might sound cheesy, but think about it — if you and your significant other got into fights because he or she was always messy, you could assume that neatness matters to you in a relationship. This can apply to any aspect of your relationship — did your ex like to go out while you liked to stay home? Did both of you like to go and do different things and not spend time with each other? Figuring out what went wrong helps you to figure out what kind of partner you are and what you want in a partner. You might find out along the way that you were not perfect in the relationship, either. That is all right, too. This reflection can also allow you to improve yourself as a partner.

Depending on how long you were with your ex before you broke up, you might have memories to go through as you try to figure out where things went wrong. Granted, you might have trouble figuring this out even if your relationship only lasted months. With that in mind, here are some questions, based on what relationship expert Susan J. Elliott formulated for you to think about as you reflect on your relationship. You do not have to answer all these questions at once. Read the questions over, think about them, and then come up with answers. Writing down the answers is not required, but it will give you time to reflect on them. Do not worry if you feel embarrassed about writing down the answers — you can always change them. Take time to answer these, but try to aim for no more than a week.

- What are six things your ex did for you during your relationship that you liked?

- What did your friends and family like about your ex? Were they the same things you liked?

- What were the positive points of the relationship?

- What were the special moments in the relationship?

- What did your family and friends not like about your ex? Did you agree with them or disagree with them? Did you make any excuses for your ex's behavior to your family?

- What were your ex's negative qualities, or qualities you wanted to change?

- What were the worst times in your relationship, not including the breakup?

- What were some of your ex's good qualities that, over time, became qualities you did not like?

- Can you think of any incidents in the relationship that should have been warning signs that you two were not getting along? If yes, what did you do about them? How did you justify staying with your ex despite these negative traits?

- Were there any problems in the relationship you can trace back to your issues?

- Is there anything in the relationship you wish you could take back?

- What do you feel your ex did wrong in this relationship?

- What do you feel you did wrong in the relationship?

- What were the times in the relationship when you or your ex hurt the other?

- If you could say anything to your ex and your ex had to listen, what would you say?

After you have had a chance to review these questions, stop. Put them away, and do not think about it. Then, go back and look at the list. Ask yourself what was special to you during this relationship and what hurt. If you come across something you no longer consider worthwhile to include, scratch it off. If something stands out to you as important, underline it, circle it or do whatever you want to make sure it stands out.

Last, try to sum up the relationship. Again, you might want to write this down to have your thoughts down. Describe what you thought about the relationship. Was it passionate or reserved? Did you like to discuss things or do more activities? Can you sum up the type of relationship you had in a word, such as sporty (playing sports or going on morning runs), academic (discussing scientific theories over coffee), physical (touching, cuddling, and kissing), or geeky (going to comic book conventions together)? Then describe how you feel about your ex. Talk about his or her good and bad points. Next, write down the things in the relationship for which you were thankful, things that still make you feel mad or upset, and things you did that you think you should apologize for. Last, write down what you miss about that relationship.

Then put the paper away. Now you have a better idea of what your relationship was like and what you would like out of future relationships. This will help as you move forward into a new relationship.

CASE STUDY: THOUGHTS FROM A DATING COACH

As a dating coach, Loxie Gant has helped people get back up and find love again. She has written articles and has agreed to share her thoughts on getting over a breakup.

It is easy for us to pretend we are over someone, but there are unanswered questions and second guesses. Save the money you would spend on a shrink and go buy a cute new journal at your favorite bookstore. Pick up a pen before you go to bed (or whenever you are feeling sad) and write it out. The process of writing and then going back and reading it later is an amazing way to relieve that weight from your shoulders. It can even be helpful to write a faux letter to your ex that you would never give them. It helps to blow off steam and can be good for the soul.

While we are in relationships, it is easy to lose focus on the things that make us happy. Make a "Me List" of the activities, hobbies and passions that make up who you are. Maybe even add in the things that you wish to accomplish in the near future. Write it out and then tape it on your mirror, next to your computer screen, or on the fridge. You are single, and it is time to put the focus back on you and do what you want.

Indefinite periods of time define chapters of our lives. One way to shake things up for women is to change your look or style. A simple hairstyle or hair color change might be the jump-start you need. If you look different on the outside, you will begin to feel different on the inside. Another option is splurging on a hot new pair of stilettos to wear on your next girls' night out. This will add a spark to your strut. In the famous words of Carrie Bradshaw, "The fact is, it's hard to walk in a single woman's shoes. That's why we need special ones now and then to make the walk a little more fun."

Setting Goals

It is good to have an idea of what you want romantically, but there is more to your life than just dating. While you are taking stock of your relationship and determining what you want in a partner, take this opportunity to look at your life and rededicate yourself to get what you want. You will want to use your journal to get the most out of this segment.

First, you need to assess where you are in life. Divide a sheet of paper into two columns, then label one side "good" and the other "bad." On the good side, write down everything you like about your life. This can include, "loving parents," or "doing well at school." Even things, such as "fan of a football team," can be added. It is your list. On the bad side, list the parts of your life you do not like, such as " have not traveled overseas," "am not famous," or "am not making enough money." When you are done, set the list aside and come back to it. Reevaluate your answers and make sure you have an accurate assessment of your life.

For the next step, turn to a new page in your journal. Then, over the course of the next week, list everything you would like to do in life. Do not limit yourself to only the things you think are within reach. If you want to own a mansion, write it down. If you would like to drive a Lamborghini, write it down. There are goals that do not depend on being rich and famous. You might want to be a black belt in karate, or vacation in Europe, or have a fulfilling career. Here is a sample list for you:

- Have a drawing career
- Be able to afford a sports car
- Live in Seattle, Washington
- Learn to fence
- Visit Italy
- Go to a good college

Again, leave your list alone. Then go back and look at it again. Mark the items that are especially important, cross out the items that on reflection are not as important as you first thought, and if you have any new items, add them. If you are feeling organized, you might even want to arrange the goals by order of importance, creating an A-list of goals, a B-list and a C-list. The main point once you have this list is to type it up and save it. Print out a copy and put it in your wallet. Take out the list and look at it on occasion.

Once you are finished with the list, accomplish the goals on it. This is the easiest item and the most difficult. It is easy because there are ways to achieve your goals, but it is difficult because you might be talking about achieving long-term goals, so you will have to be patient and deal with the occasional setback.

To get started on this list of life goals, select one goal. Try to make it a goal that is well defined, easy to achieve, or important to you. If you put "visit Italy" on your list, the first thing to do is gather information. How much does a trip to Italy cost? Where do you want to go in Italy? Who will you go with? How long do you want to stay there? What will you need to have to get to Italy, other than a plane ticket? Give yourself a time limit on when you will have the information collected, then start making a plan.

One of the problems with making a plan is trying to figure out the best way to begin. Trying to figure out the best place to start can paralyze people into postponing their goals indefinitely. There is one question that can crystallize things for you. Ask yourself, "What can I do right now to get me closer to my goal?" This question automatically orients your mind to working on your goal and attacking the most immediate step. Once you have that step in mind, work on it. If you apply this to visiting Italy, you will have to apply for a passport, so do that. Another step is to start saving money, so put away a set amount each week. Another step is to come up with an itinerary or try learning Italian.

Last, review your goal every day. This will keep your goal fixed in your mind and inspire you to work on it. While it might sound cheesy, one of the biggest reasons people do not achieve their goals is that they lose sight of what they want to do. Achieving a goal takes constant effort, and you will be more likely to put in that effort if you keep reminding yourself of the goal.

THE POWER OF LISTS — AND DETERMINATION

You have never heard of Zora Colakovic, which is understandable. She is not a celebrity, not a politician and not rich. However, Zora is one of the best examples of people making a list of life's goals and sticking with it.

When Zora was a child, she wanted to be an adventurer hero. She made a list of all the skills an adventure hero would need, such as chemistry, parachuting, mountain climbing, driving evasively, archery, knife throwing, martial arts, helicopter and airplane piloting, emergency medicine, scuba diving and demolitions.

Zora mastered the items on her list and achieved incredible things while doing so. She applied herself in school and graduated from high school when she was 15. Three years later, she earned a Bachelor of Arts degree and completed her Ph.D. coursework when she was 21. Today, Zora is an international private investigator and bounty hunter.

She is a real-life adventure hero, like she dreamed of being when she was a child. What stands out about this story is not that Zora has racked up a list of mind-blowing achievements; rather, it is that outside this list, she is not extraordinary. Her parents were not wealthy, she does not have a Mensa-level IQ score and she did not suffer any type of Bruce Wayne-level event in her childhood that set her on this path.

It is amazing what you can do if you want to do it.

Chapter 9

Finding and Meeting New People

You have made tremendous progress so far. Now you are starting to want to get out again and talk to people, to put yourself in a position where you can find someone else who will love you. The only question is, how do you do that?

Granted, there are people who have no problem getting out and meeting people. Even if you are a social butterfly, however, it can be hard to get back into the social scene, especially if you have spent weeks, months, or years with your ex. Now you have to walk up to people — even strangers — and try to make polite conversation with them to establish a new connection. If you are not someone who felt comfortable doing this beforehand, you might be experiencing a sinking feeling in your stomach as you realize you have to start the process over again.

Do not despair. It is not hard to get out and meet new people, and strike up a conversation. This chapter will guide you through the basics of meeting people and starting up a conversation. From there, it is up to you.

Body Language

One of the biggest barriers to conversation happens before words are exchanged. People who wonder why no one wants to talk to them have body language that inadvertently tells people to keep their distance. Although you have 10 seconds to get someone's attention when starting a conversation, you might not be aware that you only have three seconds to form a good first impression. Just by looking at your body language, another person will be able to immediately tell if you are approachable for conversation or if you would rather be left alone. According to several studies, the latest one Hickson, Stacks, and Moore performed in 2004, nonverbal communication amounts for anywhere from 63 percent to 93 percent of the information transmitted while talking.

Nonverbal communication is rule-based, and the rules vary with each culture. Americans are unlikely to grasp the subtleties of the Japanese bow, and Italians who visit the United States learn that Americans have a wider area of personal space than Italians. Even if you think that the subtleties of non-verbal communication are not worth memorizing, odds are that you shake hands with someone you meet for the first time and dress nicely for

Thanksgiving dinner. When you wear a T-shirt and jeans to a rock concert, you are engaging in nonverbal communication.

Nonverbal communication is ingrained and performed unconsciously, so the good news is that you can intentionally use nonverbal communication to make yourself appear friendly, sociable and a good listener. Just as you can select the kind of clothes that will make the best impression at an interview, you can employ body language that will make people want to come and talk to you.

Good body language is open and inviting and makes people more receptive to the idea of going up and talking to you. Despite the name, body language is not a new language to be mastered, like sign language. Everyone uses body language, whether they realize it or not. When you smile while watching television, for instance, you are communicating that you are happy about the show being broadcast. When you scowl at the cup you are holding, you are signaling that you do not like the taste of the coffee.

All you have to do to create body language that invites communication is to be aware of five or six simple techniques.

Smile to be approachable

The first technique is the easiest — smile. Smiling indicates friendliness, implies openness to meeting other people, and sends out a nonverbal invitation for other people to smile back. If that were not enough of a draw for other people, a smile is also an implied compliment. So the next time you are at a party and see someone you want to talk with, simply smile at them.

Frowning, on the other hand, is a warning message. So is looking serious or deep in thought. When you are frowning or looking deep in thought, you are giving off signals that you do not want anyone to talk to you.

How should you smile at someone? After studying smiling techniques, conversationalist Leil Lowndes came up with one method she believes trumps the rest. When you see someone, do not immediately break into a smile. Instead, stare at the person for a second. Take their measure, as your grandparents might have said. Then let a smile spread across your face. This works better than flashing a quick smile at someone because it gives the other person the impression that your smile is meant exclusively for him or her. It is a flattering assumption, and it will make him or her feel good about talking to you as long as the conversation lasts.

Keep your chin up

A corollary to smiling is keeping your chin up, which lets that smile you are wearing be broadcast to the rest of the crowd and makes you appear more confident. The next time you are at party, look at the most charismatic people in the room. You will see that their chins are up, and they are welcoming all conversation.

A good way to practice keeping your chin up is to look at the foreheads of other people in the room. The natural inclination for most people is to keep their eyes at eye level, but staring at forehead level has a difference most people cannot detect. It will keep your chin up and make your smile more inviting. As an added bonus, it will also make you appear more confident, which is attractive to people looking for someone to engage in conversation.

Welcome them with open arms

Another nonverbal signal that shows you are approachable is having your arms open. Although crossing your arms might be comfortable, it sends out a strong signal to the rest of the world that you are annoyed or angry. Drop your arms to your sides or have an excuse to keep them away from your body. You will be sending out a cannot-miss, nonverbal, welcoming gesture.

This information can seem counterintuitive. Some people try to get others to approach them by looking as though they are lost in thought or pondering the truths of the universe. This posture entails crossing one's arms or putting a hand to one's chin. The hope is that someone will approach and ask what you are thinking about, and a deep, meaningful conversation can ensue based on the initial deep thought. This posture has the opposite effect — people will assume you are thinking about something, but they will not want to interrupt you because you are thinking.

The habit of crossing your arms can be strong. To break it, keep one hand occupied. Get a drink and carry it around, or get a small plate of appetizers. Girls have an advantage here if they have a small strapless purse, which they can use the same way as a drink to stop their arms from crossing. You might also try to prevent your arms from crossing by sticking your hands in your pants pocket, but that will trap your arms to your sides and signal that you are closed off.

Other tricks for keeping your arms open include:

- Hitching your thumbs to your belt loops (popular among cowboys and in the country)

- Draping your jacket over one arm (this works best when outdoors)

- Putting a hand on your hip (this is mostly for women)

- Carrying a pen (also a conversation starter)

This leads into the next technique for good body language: touch. Although excessive touching is frowned on in society, some initial touching is polite, especially in the form of a handshake. The next time you go to talk to someone, stick out your hand and offer it for the other person to shake. They will naturally respond with their corresponding hand, and you will have made a connection.

Once you have established that you are receptive to talking with someone, focus on body language that lets people know you are interested in what they have to say. This can be accomplished by something as simple as leaning forward. When you are sitting next to another person who is talking to you, leaning forward indicates that you are interested in the other person and what he or she is saying. It encourages the other person to keep talking, secure in the knowledge that you appreciate what he or she is talking about. This can be counterintuitive for most people, who like to lean back while talking to someone else, especially during long conversations, to relax. However, this posture signals to your conversation partner that you are not interested in what he or she has to say or that you are not taking what he or she has to say seriously.

When you are leaning forward, do not lean in far. At best, it will look awkward, and at worst, you will be invading the other person's personal space. Sit or stand with your back straight, to start with. From there, lean forward. Practice this by yourself to have this posture look natural. If you are at a table with someone else, you are in luck. Instead of worrying how far too far is, lean forward and rest on your arms to signify interest.

During a conversation, also nod occasionally to show understanding and agreement. Nodding also signals approval, so the person you are talking to will feel that you approve of what he or she is saying. However, moderate your nodding. You do not want to come off looking like a Bobblehead.

THE GOOD BODY LANGUAGE GUIDE

- Smile at people.

- Keep your arms open and inviting.

- Shake hands to establish physical contact.

- Lean forward while someone is talking to show you are interested.

- Nod occasionally.

- Keep eye contact — but do not overdo it.

Ritual Questions and Conversation Starters

The easiest way to get someone's attention is through a "ritual" question, also known as an icebreaker — a tried-and-true method of getting a quick piece of information that also communicates a desire to learn more about the person to whom you are talking. There are three types of ritual questions, which can easily draw another person into a conversation.

The first type of ritual question works by noticing something the person is carrying, such as a book, pet, or sport or fashion accessory. Ask a ritual question that requires the other person to give you some information that relates to that item, such as, "What breed of dog is he?" or "Where do you play tennis?"

These questions can be applied to anything the person is carrying. Some items, such as musical instruments, are an invitation to ask the person how long they have been playing, the kind of music they like to play and their favorite artist. Other items, such as photographs, are more subtle because they are more personal to the person. Regardless, asking a ritual question based on something someone is carrying is not meant to pry or obtain information. It is a way to show interest in the person.

A second type of ritual question depends on the situation you find yourselves in. If you are at a dance, ask the other person what they think of the music or the kind of music they like. If you are at a non-franchise restaurant and are waiting in line with someone else, ask what he or she thinks of the restaurant's food and whether he or she has any recommendations.

This type of ritual question can be combined with the first type of ritual question, particularly if you are at a movie theater or bookstore. Asking what someone is reading is an excellent conversation starter, as is asking about his or her taste in movies.

Another way to use this type of ritual question is to offer assistance to someone, provided that they need it. Mention that they look as though they need help first, then offer your assistance. As an example, say you live in neighborhood with your family and you see someone unpacking his or her car and taking suitcases into the house next door. You could say, "I noticed you looked like you needed some help unpacking your car. I live in this neighborhood. Would you like me to help you out?" Alternately, you could start by asking if he or she is moving in and say, "I happen to live here, too. Let me help you with unloading, and I can tell you about the area while we are working."

If you cannot think of anything else, a ritual question good in any situation is to ask someone whether they are new in the area. This results in a good conversation starter because you can then ask them how long they have lived in the area or what brought them there.

The third kind of ritual question is to focus on something interesting about the other person. This is one of the most useful types of ritual questions because it could be anything: the latest smartphone model, a nice piece of clothing or dress, or a hairstyle. This ritual question is sure to get anyone talking to you as long as you start with a compliment. Unfortunately, a question about something can be perceived as a compliment or insult, and the reaction of people who are not sure why you are asking about something is to give a guarded response. A compliment gives the other person a clear signal that you like whatever it is you have noticed and that you are interested in learning more.

Some ritual questions, based on the above points of interest, could go as follows:

- "You have a smartphone. I've been wanting one of those. What do you like best about this model?"

- "That is such a nice dress. Where did you buy it?"

- "I like your tie. Where did you get it?"

- "That is a nice hairstyle. How long did it take to get it done?"

All these questions, in addition to taking less than 10 seconds to ask, have another thing in common — they are open-ended. They cannot be answered by a simple "yes" or "no," the way close-ended ritual questions can.

Here are some sample open-ended questions:

- What is the best part of that book you are reading?

- What was the first song you ever heard by your favorite band?

- What is your favorite radio station?

- What is the best coffee shop in the city?

- What is your favorite movie?

- What is the geekiest thing you have ever done?

- Have you ever gotten involved as a volunteer?

- What is your favorite school subject?

- What was the last concert you went to?

- Where would you most like to travel?

- What is the most radical change you have made to your hair?

- What is your favorite kind of ride at an amusement park?

- What is the best sightseeing attraction in the United States?

If you are not used to holding a conversation, you might feel you are intruding on someone by asking an open-ended question. In truth, however, people like sharing information about themselves. It makes them feel important. Also, people can give an indication of how willing they are to talk when they answer these questions. If someone gives short answers even if you ask an open-ended question, it is a clear signal that he or she does not want to talk. On the other hand, if someone gives a long answer to a close-ended question, you can rest assured that he or she would like to talk with you.

Abstract and Concrete Language

If you feel you are saying the wrong thing when trying to instigate a conversation, adjust your language to be more concrete. Abstract language, which refers to principles and ideas without being specific, can be confusing when two people do not share common experiences. For example, if you ask someone you just met whether he or she wants to hang around, you will get a lukewarm response or an outright rejection. This is because you are using language that is too abstract. On the other hand, if you ask a friend if he or she wanted to hang out, he or she would know what the two of you do when you hang out, such as playing ping-pong or watching movies and having pizza.

Using concrete language and specific examples is the best way to overcome this hurdle. Instead of asking someone if they want to do something fun, specify what it is you have in mind. For instance, "I was thinking of playing some Frisbee, then walking down to the ice cream booth and getting some ice cream," is a specific example that will get someone interested, even if they do not like ice cream.

HELLO, MY NAME IS...

At some point in the conversation, you are going to need to introduce yourself. This is not easy information to work into a conversation, which is ironic when you think about how important a name is to someone.

Introducing yourself at the start of a conversation is acceptable, but it can be awkward. There are few good segues from an introduction to a conversation topic, and it smacks of the elementary school greeting, "Hi, my name is so-and-so. Will you be my friend?" A child can get away with that kind of honest desperation, but as a young adult, you cannot be that emotionally open with a stranger.

The best way to introduce yourself is to do it early on in the conversation, when it is your turn to speak. After the other person has finished, say, "By the way, my name is..." and tell them. The other person will introduce himself or herself in return, and then you can get back to the topic at hand.

Once you get someone's attention, you have 20 seconds to keep it. What do you say after the initial back-and-forth talk of open-ended and close-ended questions? And what do you say when the other person asks you an open-ended question in return? This section is going to walk you through the transition from introductory conversation into full-on small talk, including when to switch from small talk to more personal conversation.

Why make small talk?

Small talk starts with the first round of introductory questions and answers, and it continues until the point where one party starts to deepen the conversation by revealing some personal details. People tend to look down on small talk and see it as a barrier to getting to know people, but it is a useful tool to have in your communications portfolio. Making small talk encourages the meaningful kinds of conversation people are hungry for in several ways.

First, small talk serves as a social litmus test for whether a person wants to talk or not. If a person answers a question in short sentences or with "yes" or "no" answers, he or she is not interested in talking with you.

Once people in a conversation have signaled that they want to talk, small talk lets you and the other person feel each other out and determine whether you want to talk to the person, and once you have decided to continue the conversation, exchange basic information about yourselves. In the process, you can establish what common ground you have. In the course of revealing this information, you are also likely to reveal topics that you are interested in, and if you listen carefully, you can tell what those topics are and talk about them in the course of the conversation. Small talk is a gateway to meaningful conversations people dream of having.

Listen to me

One of the fears of making small talk with someone is that you will have nothing to say. There you are, listening to someone talk about the goatherd his grandmother has, and when he or she finishes, you realize you have no idea what to say back. What can you say in return that you and he or she will find relevant?

If you find yourself in this situation, you were suffering from a fairly common conversational affliction — not paying attention to what the other person was saying. Instead, the moment he or she started talking about the goatherd, you thought to yourself, "So his grandmother has a goatherd. What do you say to someone who's just said that his grandmother has a goatherd?" Instead of listening to what your new friend had to say, you had focused all your attention on worrying about what to say, leaving you at a loss when it was your turn to speak. This is common with shy or scared people, so if this has happened to you, do not worry. Learn to listen actively to pick up on pieces of information you can use to continue the conversation.

Active listening is a part of making small talk. When you listen actively, you are signaling that you are taking the conversation and the other people in it seriously. They will participate more in the conversation as a result, and everyone will benefit.

Part of active listening comes from practicing good body language. Leaning forward, maintaining eye contact and nodding to show you understand what is being said. The other part of active listening has to do with knowing what you are listening for.

The first step in being an active listener is making a conscious effort to become one. When talking with someone, tell yourself you are going to actively listen to him or her. Remind yourself you are going to focus on the information he or she is giving to you. That will put you in the correct frame of mind.

Second, eliminate background noise. No matter who you are talking to, having a conversation is easier when there is no background noise interfering with your ability to listen and your thought process. Loud music, television and other conversations can distract you from the person on whom you are supposed to be concentrating. To cut down on background noise, try to find a quieter area. Sometimes this is not possible, like when you are at a party and trying to speak over the music. In this situation, the best thing you can do is to have a starter conversation and then arrange to continue the conversation afterward. Related to background noise is physical stress. You will have a hard time paying attention to someone if you are tired.

Information trapping

While you are listening to someone else speak in a conversation, you will want to be aware of the personal information he or she is giving to you. The information can be used to discover what interests you have in common, then use those interests to carry on the conversation.

Be on the alert for these types of personal information:

- Hobbies
- Favorite sports teams
- Family members

- Friends
- Books they like to read
- Recent movies they have watched
- Exercise habits
- Favorite food
- Where they live
- Neighbors
- Goals
- College they plan on attending
- Pets
- Religion

These items are a sampling of personal information that someone will reveal about himself or herself in a conversation.

When someone reveals information that you want them to talk about further, ask a question about what they were saying. Journalists refer to this as asking a follow-up question, and while an interviewee might not like being pressed for information, the people you are talking with will.

The best follow-up questions to ask are open-ended. This keeps the attention firmly on the person you are talking to, and lets him or her know you are interested in what he or she has to say. You can also use a close-ended question if he or she says something you do not understand or that seems unclear. A close-ended type of question also lets your conversation partner know you are listening, but too many close-ended questions in a row can appear you are grilling him or her, or that you were not paying close attention.

CASE STUDY: GETTING OVER YOUR EX AND STARTING TO MOVE ON

As a licensed psychotherapist in southern California with more than 30 years of counseling experience and the author of 13 books on relationships, Dr. Tina Tessina has earned her alias as "Dr. Romance." Here she shares some advice on spending time with your ex and getting ready to move on. If your ex is mean or belligerent toward you, Dr. Tessina recommends keeping a cool head and following this set of guidelines:

Choose your battles. One of my clients once said, "I don't want to die on that hill." She meant, "That battle isn't worth what it will cost me; I'll ignore that problem and save it for a bigger one." Do not get into hostile situations with your ex when it is not necessary. Even if he or she drives you crazy, do not be oppositional. Save your energy for the big issues.

Do not react, respond. Think carefully about what you say before you say it. Calculate your words to get the response you want from your ex, rather than creating a problem you will have to clean up later. It works better to deal with difficult exes by phone message or email, rather than in person. Everyone stays calmer.

You have fought your battle. It came out however it did, now let it go. You once chose this partner, and you have things to learn about your choices. Focus on learning your lessons, and do not re-fight the old battles that are already settled.

As you go through the grieving process, Dr. Tessina has five pieces of advice to help you move on emotionally:

1. If you gave it your best shot and you know it is over, do not waste time in resentment and anger; it is self-destructive. Let go. Do your grieving, cry, journal and talk about it with a trusted friend. Have a "letting go" ceremony with close friends, and say goodbye to your relationship. Put reminders away for a while.

2. If you feel you really need it, do not hesitate to get therapy to help you through this transition, so you can grieve over what is lost (even if you are the one who left, you have lost your hopes and dreams for this relationship) and move your focus on building a good life in your new circumstance. A professional viewpoint will help you move from past to present and plan for the future.

3. This is an important time to have your friends or family around you; you need support. Do not isolate yourself. You do not have to go right out and date again — go slow — but have a social life with friends and family. Even if you do not think you feel ready to see people, see your closest friends and spend time with them. They will help you heal and will remind you that you still have people who love you. Spend time with people you trust.

4. Focus on building your life. This is a time to try something other than a relationship — take a dance class, or foster a puppy. Give yourself time to heal before taking another chance on love.

Last, as you end the grieving process, keep in mind Dr. Tessina's recommendations on how to let go of the pain the dissolution of your relationship has caused.

If your relationship ends, you lose more than just your partner. Even if your relationship had problems, or you were the one who wanted out, you still will have grief over the dreams and hopes that have died with the relationship. The overwhelming feeling of loss can be confusing and difficult to understand. The following tips will help you move through these feelings and begin to focus on the future.

1. Get support: The people around you will express conflicting feelings because they are experiencing shock and loss, too. This might be a time when you find out who your true friends are. Some of your friends will avoid dealing with you or choose your ex. You need trusted friends, family, and a church or support group who will care about you, listen to you, and not judge or try to get you to "get over it."

2. Talk or write it out: Talk and write until you have expressed your grief, loss, anger, confusion and disappointment. Assume you have a specific number of tears to shed, and the more you express your feelings, the quicker you will come to the end of tears. Expressing your grief might be more than your support system wants to hear. A support group, clergy person, or therapist will be able to listen without judging until you have said everything you need to say.

3. Have a ceremony: When you feel ready, create a ceremony for letting go of your grief. You might want to include some of your close friends, destroy a memento that symbolizes your grief or the lost relationship and share your hopes for the future.

Finding common interests

You can ask almost anything you want, but the best questions to ask are on subjects the other person feels passionately about and about interests they have in common with you. Discussing common interests forms an instant bond between you and the other person. It is also a ready-made topic for small talk. You can easily spend a conversation talking about one interest both of you share.

Conversations also run smoother if everyone involved is talking about a topic that interests them. Think back to a time you have had a successful conversation with someone. Odds are that you were discussing a topic with the other person that you felt strongly about or enjoyed. You were not worrying about whether the person you were talking with found you interesting or how to keep the conversation going. New topics based on that common interest presented themselves naturally, and you and the other person smoothly segued from one aspect of your common interest to the next with as much ease as walking. Talking about your passions is easier than talking about subjects you are unfamiliar with.

What do you do with the information once you have it?

Now you know something about the person with whom you are talking. You know where he or she lives, where he or she goes to school and maybe even a hobby or two. You might also be wondering what to do with this information now that you have it.

The answer is simple: Learn more about the person. Take one of the topics or pieces of personal information you have learned and ask the other person about it. At this stage of the conversation, pick and choose a topic that interests you, and have options available. Ask open-ended questions about what you have learned and throw in close-ended questions for clarification.

The Building Blocks of a Romantic Relationship

Most romantic relationships begin the same way friendly relationships do. People in close proximity to each other form bonds over time and progress from casual acquaintances to nascent friends and then stabilized friends. A romantic relationship, though, has three aspects working together that are not found in other kinds of relationships. These aspects mix together in different ways and create what are known as love styles, or ways that people express their love for each other.

The first aspect of a relationship is **passion**. Passion is an intense desire for and positive feelings about the other person. It generates the emotional high you get when you fall in love with someone. Passion is responsible for the sparks in a relationship and the emotional highs you get from being in love. However, passion is inconstant. Passion ebbs and flows, and as a result, a relationship built on passion alone cannot last.

Commitment is a second aspect of the relationship and is the counterpart to passion. Although passion is a subconscious emotional decision that can come and go, commitment is a conscious choice. A decision to commit is based on the reward that continuing a relationship offers. The most common symbol of commitment is found in marriages, in particular, during the "for better or for worse" vows. Among the rewards committing to a relationship offers is the level of emotional support and the companionship the other person offers.

Underpinning passion and commitment is **intimacy**. When you feel intimate in a relationship, you feel close to the other person and a strong personal connection. Intimacy and passion are closely tied. When you feel passionate for someone, you also feel strongly about him or her, which increases feelings of intimacy. This is why passionate encounters are mistakenly assumed to generate more intimacy. However, intimacy does not ebb and flow as wildly as passion does. Intimacy is ongoing and abiding. It is the feeling that romantic partners have for each other even when they do not feel passionate. In addition, when you commit to a long-term relationship, you are consciously choosing to increase your intimacy with your partner.

Love styles

The importance that each of the three dimensions of love plays in an individual's perception of love varies. According to research John Alan Lee performed in 1973 and 1988, people express their love in one of three primary styles. Lee's research also uncovered secondary styles of how people express their love. These secondary styles are based on mixtures of the primary styles.

Eros love is the most passionate kind of love that can persuade you to ask out that cute person waiting in line behind you at the grocery store — it is intuitive and spontaneous. A person who expresses his love in the eros style falls in love with someone, and he falls hard. He expresses his love early on to his partner, and the intensity of his love transcends the physical aspects and easily encompasses spiritual and intellectual aspects of love.

A similar kind of primary love style is **ludus** love, which is more like a game to see whether you can get someone to fall in love with you and enjoy the feeling of falling in love with someone else. However, a deeper connection is not the ultimate aim of ludic love. Instead, the fun is in the chase, in playing the field. Ludic lovers are also more romantic. In a study that will shock no one, Clyde and Susan Hendrick discovered that men tend to express their love more ludically than women.

Women express their love more through the style of **storge**, the practical, sensible car in contrast to the exciting sports car that is erotic love. It is expressed gradually, and as opposed to the difficulties of erotic love, storgic love has a higher amount of stability and is more peaceful than eros love. This is perhaps the most common kind of love to come out of friendships because storgic love surfaces through discovering that you and your romantic partner have similar goals, enjoy similar things and have similar values. Storgic love is not as intense as love in the eros style, but storgic love will not suffer the crashing conflicts that eros love can bring.

Another love style that women express is the **pragma** style of love, the first of the secondary love styles and the result of mixing storgic love with ludic love. Pragmatic lovers might seem cold and calculating at first because they have clear stipulations about with whom they fall in love. This type of love uses the storgic lover's sensibility and security and the strategizing ludic lovers use when playing the field. Pragmatic lovers believe that true, enduring love is the result of making sure partners are compatible before agreeing to fall in love. Pragmatic love is the foundation for an arranged marriage.

The polar opposite of pragma love is **mania** love, a love style that many of you teens exhibit and a potent blending of eros and ludus styles. Low self-esteem fuels this love style, and a manic lover tends to be unsure if he or she is loved. The eros style of loving drives him or her to extreme highs and lows, while the ludic part of this love style leads him or her to evaluate a partner's love and commitment to him or her through games or tests. A manic lover can feel so strongly about his or her relationship that he or obsesses over it.

Last, there is **agape** love, a love that is considered so pure that people feel that it is unattainable. Agape love comes from two love styles — eros and storge — and means an agapic lover feels an intense passion toward his or her partner and feels this passion consistently. This kind of love is known for its selflessness and generosity. An agapic lover feels his or her best when his or her partner is happy and willingly ensures his or her partner is happy even if his or her efforts are not returned. Although purely agapic lovers are rare, people who express their love display agapic love to their partners.

Most people do not have one specific love style. Instead, they use a blend of primary and secondary love styles. Someone might be pragmatic when initially selecting a romantic partner and then be erotic throughout the relationship with a strong undercurrent of storgic stability. Also, love styles can change as people develop relationships and as they learn from previous ones. Your love style can also change as a result of your partner's love style. Your love style is not good or bad. What matters is how your love style connects with your partner's style.

Mingling With Singles

Now that you know about love styles, you are ready to take on the singles scene in whatever part of the world you are in. When you go to a place to make new and potentially romantic connections, you are being as vulnerable as possible. According to conversation expert Debra Fine, no one likes to admit he or she is specifically looking to connect with someone. Starting a conversation with someone is easier if you have an excuse, such as being at a school event. Despite this, talking with another single person is similar to talking with anyone else. The basic conversation techniques still apply, and it is just a matter of tweaking them to fit the situation.

Making your entrance

When you go to an event single, do not feel you need to come in talking the first moment you enter the door. Instead, center yourself. Make sure you feel calm in whatever way works for you. Then, take one step through the door and, unless you are part of a line, stop and survey the situation. Be sure you continue to use relaxed, open body language. This will call attention to you, and it will also frame you as a self-confident person who is not afraid of attention. This will set you apart from the crowd, and it might entice people to come and talk with you instead of you having to make the first move.

After you have announced your presence, though, make an effort to blend in with the crowd. Do not feel you need to be the life of the party. Instead, wander through the crowd. As you are doing so, get a sense of what the gathering is like. Are people excited or laid back? Does the mood seem formal or informal? Are people happy or stoic? Let your mind make observations, and then you can start turning those observations into icebreakers.

Impersonal icebreakers can be effective at certain events. Making an innocent remark about the event can spur someone to give his or her opinion of what is going on, and from there, you can use a ritual open-ended question to start a conversation.

How to Ask Someone On a Date

This is the whole reason you have been mingling with other singles. Someone has come along whom you connect with and who captivates you. You have talked with him or her for a while, and you want to make your move and ask him or her on a date.

For most people, this is the point where the mouth-and-brain connection fails completely. You want to ask this other person on a date in a way that is meaningful yet casual, sincere yet smooth, and uses the right words so the other person will accept your offer. Also, there is the small matter that you are putting your ego on the line and risking the fact that you will be turned down, perhaps publicly, which is embarrassing. With that kind of pressure riding on the phrasing of one request, it is no wonder that many times people get tongue-tied. The best that they can come up with is, "Want to go out on a date next Saturday?" The main problem with this way of asking someone out is that, regardless of how much time you have spent talking to the other person, asking him or her out seems to come out of the blue, without any lead up.

When asking someone out on a date, do not ask the person if he or she wants to go out. Do not ask her what he or she is doing that Friday or Saturday night unless you have a fondness for hackneyed excuses, such as "Washing my hair." Instead, before you make the offer or call him or her on the phone, come up with some ideas about an activity this person might like to do. At this point, you might realize that to come up with these activities, actively listen to the person and keep at least a mental record of his or her likes, dislikes, personality and hobbies. In other words, you need to use the skills you use in making friends if you want him or her to respond positively to your request for a date.

RUNNING OUT THE CLOCK

When you decide to ask someone on a date, there is the question of when you should do it. Some people immediately ask someone out on a date if the first meeting goes well. Others like to wait until the second or third meeting. Some even like to wait longer than that.

Asking someone out after you have met him or her multiple times is the best policy. This gives the person a chance to know you better and develop familiarity while there is still the excitement of meeting someone new. If you ask someone out on the first meeting, you are asking him or her to judge you as a romantic prospect, in addition to judging you as a person. If you wait too long, the excitement he or she feels will die down and leaving him or her less likely to see you as someone about whom he or she feels passionate.

However, do not feel pressured to ask someone out if you are not ready. If you need more time to get to know someone, do so. Good relationships come out of people knowing each other for a while before realizing there is an attraction.

If you are asked out

Congratulations. If someone has asked you on a date, he or she obviously thinks well of you. Enjoy the ego rush, and then accept or decline as you see fit. The only rule you need to follow is this: Empathize with the person who is asking you out. Do not lead him or her on, respond rudely, or act nonchalant. After all, the other person has taken a huge risk to confess his or her feelings to you. If you act nonchalant, the other person might get the impression that you do not care about him or her or the conversation. Neither will do his or her ego any good.

Instead, be enthusiastic if you accept his or her offer. If you cannot be enthusiastic, then show your interest in the upcoming date. If you decide to decline, let him or her down gently. He or she will be embarrassed, so try to convey that you are flattered and do not feel awkward about being asked out and that you might like to be friends anyway.

This advice applies no matter which gender you are. While girls asking guys out is becoming more common, a girl has to overcome the feeling of taking a huge risk and making herself vulnerable and also the difficulty of bucking a social norm. To do that takes courage. If nothing else, respect that courage.

Chapter 10

Beginning a
New Relationship

I t is finally time. You might feel happy and confident
enough on your own, but you would like to get in
another relationship, not because you want to fill the
void left by your previous relationship or are scared that if you
do not find another date you will be the only person without
someone else. You are looking for a relationship because you
want to be in one.

Still, as the saying goes, once bitten, twice shy. Getting into a new
relationship can be hard, especially if the last one broke your
heart. You might have doubts about getting into a new relationship, such as whether the person you are dating will break your
heart the same way your ex did, or you might find yourself won-

dering if you are over your ex. You are not alone. People experience these doubts when they start dating again.

Post-breakup Dating

The first date after a breakup can be odd, emotionally speaking. Even though you are trying to concentrate on how nice the other person is and the interesting story she is telling about when she visited Paris, for some reason you realize you miss your ex, even though she never even left the country. Here are some reactions relationship expert Susan Elliott compiled that you might have on your first post-breakup dates:

I am still mourning my old relationship

Grief is a funny thing. It can surface as a reaction to moving on and signal one last sense of loss as you turn the page. Other times, it can be a sign that you are still feeling the loss of your last relationship keenly enough that you should postpone dating longer. There is no test to determine which kind of grief it is. You need to figure it out for yourself, and it might take more than one date to figure it out. Any more than three dates, though, and you can be sure the feelings of grief are residual. If you feel the need to pull back, it is not because there is something wrong with you. You will be ready to date again. Just be patient.

I am not going to find someone

When you date someone, particularly if you are trying to make a good impression, you start to become acutely aware of your shortcomings. Plus, dating is scary and difficult, no matter how nonchalant we try to be about it. This can overwhelm you, and then all you see is what is wrong — with yourself, with your date and with the situation. When this happens, the important thing is to recognize it and take a mental step back. Excuse yourself to the restroom if you have to, and then give yourself a quick pep talk.

I do not think this person likes me

If you get a sense that your date is not that into you, do not take it personally. If your date's rejection of you makes you feel bad, this might be a sign that you are not quite ready to start dating again. Give yourself a break from dating for a week or two, but look on the positive side — you had the courage to take that first step of getting back into the field.

I do not think I like this person

If you do not like your date, at least be gracious and do not end the date early unless he or she is being mean or obnoxious. After you get home, though, go through the date and try to discover what it was about the person you did not like. Is it because they shared some traits with your ex? Is it because they were different than your ex and you are out of your comfort zone? Whatever the reason, do not write off your date. You might even want to give him or her another chance, and if he or she is not for you, end things politely.

Standards and "Good Enough"

One of the problems with dating again is trying to figure out what you are looking for in a date. On the plus side, you have the experience you gained from your relationship with your ex, which should give you some perspective on what you are looking for. Your relationship with your ex is also on the negative side of the equation. If you like someone like your ex, does this mean that he or she will also break your heart the way your ex did?

As you start dating again, start evaluating your relationship with the person you are seeing. How much time do you spend together? How much time does he or she want to spend with you, versus the time you are comfortable with? How does your date react when you want to spend time with other people? These questions can be hard to ask, especially if you are lucky enough to have a date that goes well.

To properly assess how your date is going, spend time away from him or her. The best way to do that is to stick with your schedule. Keep appointments with your friends, continue working on your hobbies, and do not slack off on trips to the gym. While you are away from your new date and taking a breather from your emotions, consider what your boundaries are in this new relationship. What are you willing to compromise? What are the deal-breakers? How fast do you want this relationship to move? Once you have a sense of what you want out of this relationship, the next step is to stick to it. If your date wants you to move beyond your boundaries, politely but firmly refuse. This might lead to the end of your relationship, but in the long run, you need to be comfortable with yourself, and you are guaranteed to feel better when you refuse to compromise the principles that are important to you than you will be if you sacrifice them just to stay with someone. People in healthy relationships know what is important to them, and they know how to compromise without giving up anything important to them. You will have to practice to achieve this balance.

Standards can be too high. Do you only want to date people from wealthy families? Do you turn down people who do not look like bikini models? If so, loosen your standards. This does not mean you should completely abandon your standards, though. For instance, you want to date someone you are attracted to, and like it or not, looks do matter. When you assess whether you want to date someone, though, do not dismiss him if he does not look like a man you would find in a magazine. The same rule applies if a potential date is not as financially well off as you would like.

OBLITERATING STANDARDS

If you want to shake up your dating world, you might try to follow in the footsteps of Maria Dahvana Headley. After realizing she seemed to date the same type of guys, she decided to do an experiment. For one year, she would go out with everyone who asked her out — no exceptions. Maria wrote about her experiences in a book, The Year of Yes, and detailed about her dates with playwrights, cowboys, salsa dancers, ice cream men and how she eventually fell in love.

The opposite problem of having standards that are too high is accepting someone who is just "good enough." Everyone settles and compromises to some degree when forging a relationship, and that is to be expected. However, you do not want to be in a relationship with someone just because he or she treats you better than your ex did. By this point, you know what you want in a relationship, and you know what you are willing to compromise. You are worth having someone love you — without sacrificing what is important to you.

CASE STUDY: STRAIGHT TO THE POINT

Roy Biancalana is a relationship coach, the latest leg on a life journey that has seen him be the CEO of a nonprofit organization and a pro golfer. He has been trained by some of the top psychologists and relationship coaches in the country, and he is the author of A Drink with Legs: From Being Hooked to Being Happy — A Spiritual Path to Relationship Bliss.

Roy Biancalana is big on personal responsibility when it comes to the subject of breakups. "The first step is to feel your feelings deeply, allow it to be, and then let go of the victim mentality and take responsibility for how you contributed to the demise of the relationship. Understand that you break your own heart. You are responsible for your feelings."

One interesting aspect of Roy's philosophy behind breakups that stems from his mantra of personal responsibility is that people whose relationships fail are responsible for them. "You did this to yourself; you wanted out of the relationship — and we know that because that is what happened." This straightforward attitude differs considerably from other relationship coaches' advice.

How does this philosophy translate into counseling someone after they have gone through a breakup? "The advice I give is to tell the complete truth," Roy says. "Own your part in the relationship, let go of playing the victim, which means to stop blaming, complaining, judging, or labeling (your ex). If you have awakened to your own personal issues that contributed to the entire relationship and its demise then you would have no trouble or fear of opening your heart, for you are no longer the same person and cannot therefore create a similar result."

When dealing with an ex, Roy prefers to look past how people should act and focus on what is going on. "I don't deal in 'shoulds,'" he explains. "If (someone whose relationship has failed) is mean and nasty, then it is simply a sign that they are playing the victim and seeing the ex as a villain. When they see that they wanted the relationship to end, unconsciously, all anger and meanness dissolves by itself. And when a person goes through a breakup, they wanted it on some level."

Roy has the same no-nonsense approach when it comes to being able to date again. "Time tables are silly. You are ready to start dating when you unwind your responsibility for the breakup and when you no longer feel attachment or aversion toward your ex. That can happen within days; for others, it does not happen for decades. You have to know your issues and shift them or you will attract the same kind of person and create the same kind of relationship. So they should approach dating with fear if they have not done their work, but joy if they have."

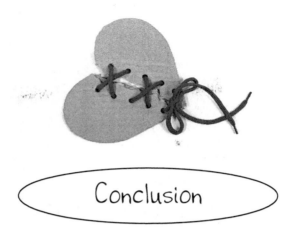

Conclusion

You are finally here. Congratulations. It has not been an easy journey, but you have gotten through your grief and accepted that your old relationship has ended. You feel good about yourself, and although you might not be completely satisfied with where you are in life, you are happy with where you are and you have some goals toward which you are working.

You are stronger than you were when you first began the book. Remember the old saying, "What doesn't kill you makes you stronger?" You have officially joined the ranks of those strengthened by adversity.

Now get out on the dating scene and enjoy yourself.

Bibliography

Baxter, Leslie. *Encyclopedia of Human Relationships*. By Harry T. Reis and Susan Sprecher. Thousand Oaks, CA: SAGE Publications, 2009. N. pag. Print.

Behrendt, Greg, and Amiira Ruotola-Behrendt. *It's Called a Breakup Because It's Broken: the Smart Girl's Breakup Buddy*. New York: Broadway, 2005. Print.

Bronson, Howard F., and Mike Riley. *How to Heal a Broken Heart in 30 Days: a Day-by-day Guide to Saying Goodbye and Getting on with Your Life*. New York: Broadway, 2002. Print.

Elliott, Susan J. *Getting past Your Breakup: How to Turn a Devastating Loss into the Best Thing That Ever Happened to You*. Cambridge, MA: Da Capo Lifelong, 2009. Print.

Piderman, Katherine. "Forgiveness: Letting Go of Grudges and Bitterness - MayoClinic.com." *Mayo Clinic Medical Information and Tools for Healthy Living - MayoClinic.com.* N.p., n.d. Web. 31 Aug. 2010. **www.mayoclinic.com/health/forgiveness/MH00131**.

Stosny, Steven. "Mad about You: Simple and Complex Jealousy | Psychology Today." *Psychology Today: Health, Help, Happiness Find a Therapist.* N.p., n.d. Web. 01 Sept. 2010. **www.psychologytoday.com/blog/anger-in-the-age-entitlement/201002/mad-about-you-simple-and-complex-jealousy**.

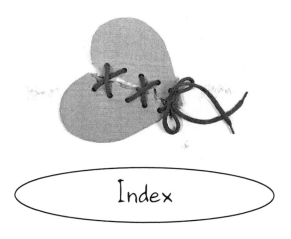

Index

R

S

T